Discover the Unseen
in business, life, and yourself

Rachel,
Enjoy the journey
and proclaim your
life! Jill

T.J. WAGONER

AudioInk Publishing
P.O. Box 1775
Issaquah, WA 98027
www.AudioInk.com

Distributed by AudioInk Publishing
Cover/Interior Design by Amy H. Avery
Artwork by Karina Cohrs
Photograph by Taylor Rubart
Writing Consultant: Olivia H. Montgomery

Library of Congress Cataloging-in-Publication data

> Wagoner, T.J.
> Discover the Unseen: In Business, Life and Yourself
> p. cm.
> ISBN: 978-1-61339-657-5
> L.C.C.N. 2014934092
> 1. SELF-HELP / Personal Growth / General
> 2. BUSINESS & ECONOMICS / Personal Success
> 3. SELF-HELP / Personal Growth / Success

For further information contact AudioInk +14255266480 or email support@AudioInk.com

I find it impressive that Jeff has been able to distill his life experiences, even in their evolution, into this system of processes by which he can help others to self-discovery. Seekers will find it an interesting journey to a future of satisfaction with self and others.

— *Laurie Magers,* Executive Assistant to Zig Ziglar

"T.J. Wagoner is one of the influential thought leaders in uncovering and accentuating the potential in human beings. This book is a window into his many years of being a business practitioner serving corporations, leaders and their teams. It really doesn't matter what phase of life you are in, or where you are on the continuum of your carrier, Jeff has insight that is practical and applicable. The wisdom contained in these pages will release you to fulfill all you are meant to be. In an ever increasing world filled with challenges Jeff is on a quest to encourage and inspire those who want an extraordinary life. Don't let the opportunity to Discover the Unseen in you pass by."

— *Buzz Leonard,* Advisor IGS

"Discover the Unseen is a physical illumination of how mind and body combine to consider choices to be made. The beautiful message is one of wisdom that can be used to address all facets of one's life, professional and personal."

— *Cap Kotz,* Owner Cappy's Boxing Gym

A visceral call to action that is screaming to be heard. Advent5 works!

— *Bill Chandler,* Author of The Ultimate Inventors Handbook

"When I met Jeff he had that unusual twinkle in his eyes that somehow screamed out to my inner man and said, "You just didn't know the secret". Jeff is a perfect mixture of a spiritual and practical thinker. I am so impressed with him and his book that I have asked him to speak at our School of Generosity this upcoming year, which teaches people to earn more, save more and to give more. I am sure he will be not only be inspirational, but will empower to achieve our dreams with less energy, while experiencing much more joy while doing it.

I am sure you will not only enjoy his book, but it will become the most valuable possession you own because of the success it will bring you if acted upon."

— *Neil Schober, fitness club owner, and director of the School of Generosity at The City Church in Seattle, Washington*

"Discover the Unseen describes Jeff's amazing journey and the Advent5 Process. Anyone who reads his book will most definitely be empowered to embark on a personal, and life-changing journey of his/her own. The Advent5 Process provides the tools necessary to discover your true desires and the realization of a much greater cause. I recommend that you read the book, reflect then read it again as you begin your own transformational journey."

— *Patrick Tuttle, ADR Inc. CEO*

Do you feel like you're in a routine? Have you ever thought to yourself is there more to life then this? Jeff has a way of pulling that best out of you and getting you of your own way. This book will help you discover your best and put that best into action. Strap on your seatbelt and get ready for the ride of your life.

— *Mitch Soule, Business Owner, Success Coach, and Motivational Speaker*

Through Jeff's Advent5 weekend retreat, I was able to uncover desires buried deep within, acknowledge my limiting beliefs, recognize my talents and discover my Righteous Cause. I now have the steps needed to transform my life from living in 'survival mode', to living a life of legacy and purpose.

— *Kathy Knox, working mother of 4*

"This information in the book helped me change from wasting personal resources being in a 'could happen mindset' to enjoy the love and energy of what 'is happening' by connecting me to what I was wired to do and therefore finding a deeper fulfilment and grace for the journey "

– *Stephen MacDonald, Entrusted Business Advisor, and Professional Speaker*

"I've witness Jeff Wagoner walk people through amazing transformation going through the Advent5 process. This book has the keys to connecting your deepest desire with a cause that is bigger than yourself."

— *Bryan Heathman, Author of Conversion Marketing*

Jeff, I am amazed and inspired by your systematic yet creative approach to helping people both personally and professionally get unstuck! "Discover the Unseen" is the must-have blueprint for anyone who's ever had a great idea lurking in their mind for days, weeks, months, or years! Thank you for sharing your Advent5 Process, now everyone has access to your amazing coaching and system at a fraction of the price! It's as though you're right there walking through the process of turning dreams into reality. Thanks Jeff!

— *Dawn Jones, The Personality Motivator, Best Selling Author of Top 7 Personality Challenges*

"Jeff is a man on a mission to help people discover and awaken unique passions and dreams that are so often left dormant. 'Discover the Unseen' is an experiential read that will challenge, motivate, and assist in igniting a fire inside you to live an intentional life of purpose and meaning."

— *Joanna Balin*, Specialized Emergency Rescue and EMT Professional

Jeff's Advent5 Process could help you uncover what's been hindering your personal and professional progress. Having not only developed but lived the process, he is well suited and equipped to enable you to open doors you may have found difficult or even impossible in the past.

— *Tom Ziglar*, President, Ziglar, Inc.

"Jeff causes you to stop and take a critical and objective look at your life. He helps you get off the often preprogrammed treadmill that you are on and ask yourself if you are leading the right life for you, and then motivates you to move in a new, healthy direction."

— *Al Haase*, Aerospace and Defense CEO

"This book is the best I've ever read on finding your dream and effectively pursuing it. The writing is clear, compelling and practical. It's a must read for anyone who wants to dig up their dream, throw it down the road and pursue it with a plan. This book will change your life."

— *Bill Perkins*,
Author of:
Awaken the Leader Within
Why Naked Women Look so Good
The Jesus Experiment

Prologue

This book is my attempt to offer you the lessons, stories, concepts, and wisdom assembled through my lifelong process of self-discovery. What I am about to share with you are some of my most profound and personal experiences, and I am honored to share them with you.

Acknowledgements

There are many who have inspired me, past and present, during the writing of this book and with wonderful, enlightening self-discovery experience—so many that it would be difficult to list them all. However, I would like to especially thank those that are close to me (you know who you are) who have supported my Desire and living out my Righteous Cause. I love you all!

Thanks to <u>everyone</u> who has passed through my life. I do appreciate each and every one of you and those experiences and relationships we have shared!

I believe that imagination is stronger than knowledge. That myth is more potent than history. That dreams are more powerful than facts. That hope always triumphs over experience. That laughter is the only cure for grief. And I believe that love is stronger than death.

— Robert Fulghum

"Whoever authors your story authorizes your actions."

— Sam Keen

Contents

Preface

To be yourself in a world that is constantly trying to make you something else is the greatest accomplishment.

— Ralph Waldo Emerson

Three Magic Words

The most profound words that can be uttered on any journey of self-discovery are these three: "I need help."

At their core, these words acknowledge the Desire for a fundamental shift, and at the same time they are an admission that help is available and necessary to achieve this shift. The idea also contains within it the kernel of truth that the whole really is greater than the sum of its parts. Help is possible, and help is at hand. Whether you get the help you need from the pages of a book, a trusted friend, a network of experts, society as a whole, or from quieting your mind and listening for your inner voice, help is always at hand.

This book is intended to help you transform your life from what it is now to what you would like it to be. The process I've developed helps you connect with your inner self, the authentic self, to understand and define your Desire, to ignite emotion and engage your passion. It consists of working with five elements, each one a metaphor for a stage in the process.

My background is mainly from the corporate sector and the last 15 years center in the field of consulting, specifically business process coaching. For decades my job has been helping people solve problems. Through some experiences in my own life, I discovered that *the process can be universally applied.* It led me to create the core ideas in this book, the essence of the title *Discover the Unseen...,* and what I call the *Advent⁵ Process.* Advent⁵ is an action-driven, results-oriented process by which you participate in the design of your life. The definition of *Advent* is the coming or arrival of something extremely important, and the number 5 represents the life path plus freedom and change. Remarkably, this process is adaptable to any situation, available at any time, and limited only by you.

Stages of transformation and the overall process elements

Transformation is a process, not an event. That means we can break down the stages of transformation into a workable, predictable system of events. Transformation itself can be expressed in five stages. And, also, with the 5 Elements of Advent⁵ (Fire, Water, Wind, Sun and Rock).

Stage 1 Fire - Awakening: It all begins with an awakening, experienced as a positive motivation; the simple Desire for a better situation or way of life. This may be anything from a vague sense of dissatisfaction to a complete sense of being overwhelmed, making you want to stay in bed all day holding a pillow over your head, wishing the world would just stop spinning so you could climb off. The awakening may also be the sudden and unexpected realization that something must change, or it may show up as a **burning** passion. Whatever its form, *the awakening marks the beginning of the journey of discovery and transformation.*

Stage 2 Water - Acknowledgement: The methods in this book encourage a stoic and calm acceptance of the present situation, rather than denial. Acknowledgement allows an individual to understand the futility of resistance and denial of the status quo, and enter a more constructive state of mind. This is a *reviewing of where you are, with what you have, and who you are at this moment,* with understanding of all that you are and what is needed to align with your Desire. Acknowledgment of allowing the **flow** as it is will be the next step toward transformation. It's the realization that "I need help."

Stage 3 Wind - Acceptance: The key to fulfillment is acceptance. Without acceptance, we're naturally in a combative frame of mind, fighting against the conditions we reject. This creates an ineffective situation, one that restricts forward movement and constructive resolution. *The things we allow and accept will actually transform and the ones we resist we get to keep. What we resist persists.* It's the acceptance of what is present, even if it's perceived as unwanted, by the leaning into adversity that **blows** into your present moment with acceptance and no denial that will bring forward movement.

Some of the accepting is painful because of the ego. It's human nature to fight against conditions. The ego gets so attached to the need for certain conditions or circumstances that it gets in the way of life's own progress. Once you rise above the foreground of the day-to-day of what you see, you'll begin to see that which is the essence of you. Just as a painter needs to step back from his work from time to time to gain perspective, you need to find the still, calm center within your own life to gain a perspective of the total picture. Only then can you make clear, productive choices about your life path and your day-to-day activities.

Stage 4 Sun - Alignment: Your values, paradigms and passions must be in alignment with your goals. So many people go through life believing that the objectives they are pursuing are worthwhile. Yet when they accomplish these goals they can't understand why there is such a deep well of emptiness inside. *Aligning your pursuits and your passions* avoids costly mistakes and misdirection of time and resources. It creates a focus, and with this aligned focus your **path** will be illuminated.

Stage 5 Rock - Action: The final piece required for transformation is action. Acknowledging that you need help and accepting the emotions or conditions you're experiencing is only the start. To move beyond your current state, you must take action with accountability. The principles in this book will assist you in discovering exactly which actions to take. Not just any actions, but *actions built on a solid foundation of who you are* and what you want from your life. Adapting these stages and elements will guide you to the discovery of your purpose. This is a continual process that is **sustainable** in the present moment and into your desired out come.

The process works in a wide variety of situations, especially personal goal setting. The fundamental premise is to take a look at your current state, deconstruct it, and develop the future state by using the steps that I have outlined.

It begins with mapping out the status quo, listing everything related to it, then reviewing the activities. Anything that's a waste of time, energy or attention gets flushed out automatically. The activities that remain become the core of action in alignment with your true Desire, and the standardized path for moving forward becomes clear.

By using the present moment, here and now, you create your future. This is the simple process of causality. The idea asserts that the *future will continue like the past unless we change it in the present.* "Insanity is doing the same thing over and over again and expecting different results." This process provides a path around the insanity most of us experience in our daily lives.

All of this begins with making a choice - a choice in focus, a choice in awareness, and a choice in lifestyle. Making the choice to remove yourself from the distractions of the day-to-day world which are not in alignment with your Desire will allow you to begin focusing on living the life you are intended for.

Using the *Discover the Unseen...* ideas, concepts and processes to connect with your authentic self, you'll discover the essence of the life you Desire. Just as your perception is the foundation of your current reality, the basis of what you perceive with your senses is the foundation of physical science. The five senses sight, sound, touch, taste and scent transmit signals to the brain. These are interpreted by your thoughts, and they influence how you interpret your experiences, your beliefs, and your model for living. The Advent[5] Process allows you to reinterpret what you perceive and apply it in a new way, which allows you to reach a better understanding of your beliefs, and then align your actions with your Desire. This provides a path to achieving what you really want from life, yourself, and those around you.

Discover the Unseen…Life is full of insignificant noise and distraction. So many people live in a state of reaction, living as if on auto-pilot, with set routines and even methods for interacting with people, rather than focusing with consciousness and intent on the few key things that are really important to them. Our passions are often pushed aside to make room for society's ideas of "success," but these suppressed passions and the God-given gifts at our core make up the foundation of our purpose. You may ask yourself at this point, what is it that we <u>don't</u> see?

Looking for what you don't see is:

- ◆ Focusing on your Desire
- ◆ Believing in the unseen
- ◆ Going beyond the obvious
- ◆ Observing from the background
- ◆ Awareness of thought
- ◆ Searching within
- ◆ The true meaning of your wants
- ◆ Seeking for what is already here
- ◆ Looking past the foreground
- ◆ Understanding the Divine
- ◆ Feeling the emotion
- ◆ Moving past the situation
- ◆ Authentic truth
- ◆ Your essence
- ◆ Your Righteous Cause

The Background vs. the Foreground

Welcome to the background, the space of awareness itself. This is the place where your authentic self resides. You have nothing to fix, nothing to improve, just your Desire to discover. Here, no answers, feelings, or ideas are wrong. It is just you at your purest: a spiritual being within a human body. Your Desire awaits your focus and intention to engage. When this happens, your life begins to transform. This is when you detach from society's prescribed path for success and begin to participate in the design of your own journey. ***Every experience, decision, and event in your life has led you to this point.*** These events aren't necessarily good or bad but they are just things that have happened on your path. And everything and anybody that is needed along the way will cross your path. These are the events and people that contribute to who you are.

The foreground of the physical presence is where most of us spend the majority of our time, this daily space where temporary forms and situations come and go. They represent movement - waves that pass through this time and space, our surrounding environment. You can feel the disconnection from the background. You could say that these are elements of the distraction.

It's the background that becomes our reality. The background is what we seek: the essence of silence, the stillness, the observer of the authentic you. This is known by a lot of names, and it's not my intent to define this for you. The important thing is that you become aware of the background where your true self resides. This still, calm center is where the acceptance is found and where transformation begins.

This is the essence of the message, *"Discover the Unseen..."* Contained within it is the idea that as an individual, you don't need any fixing. *You're not broken.* You have been brought to this place by the events in your life, and everything has happened just as it should. *You are exactly where and who you need to be.*

You already have the answers, and everything you need is available for you. It's your perceptions, beliefs, fears and judgments that keep you from seeing the answers you seek. Everything you need, *everything you're looking for is here;* it's present in the here and now. The Advent[5] Process will guide you along your journey on the path of your Desire.

This is exactly what I tell myself and others: that all we need is here and now, and within us, waiting in the background. It's the searching outside for approval, acceptance, and even love that leaves us wanting, and with that sense of lack in our lives. When we seek purpose and meaning externally, we always come up empty – always! It's an emptiness that is dark and endless. Simply turn your focus, energy and seeking to the stillness within and emptiness will begin to disappear. It is the stillness that you can't name, can't create, and can't become... because it is you! That is the essence of who you truly are. *This is where you find your Righteous Cause*, the one thing that matters most in your life. When you do find it, all else seems to fall in place and life becomes simple, even magical.

An Effective, Simple, Workable Process

We might say that using this process is a bit like climbing a mountain. Many give up along the way, but there are those who succeed who provide the example for those who follow. A common failure with the process occurs when people try to climb the whole mountain or tackle the entire challenge all at once. They get overwhelmed and quit before they've even reached the half-way point. Sometimes people give up when significant progress could be seen with just a few more steps because they see the task in its entirety, and not what it is: a steady series of steps along the journey. They could be mere inches away from obtaining their true Desires, but they just don't see it through the sea of noise and distraction.

What they lack is what you have in your hands right now: an effective, simple, workable process. A good Sherpa wouldn't overload you with a year's supply of food, a dozen tents, tons of extra maps, and too many blankets. But so often people who teach problem solving skills for the life path are guilty of doing exactly that, overloading the very people they're trying to help. They give them more than they will ever need, and it bogs down progress. *It's fair to say that stuff does not equal value.* Overloaded preparation creates the path to being overwhelmed, and people give up before they get started.

Maybe you've encountered this already in other programs or other attempts to reach your desired outcome. If so, don't worry about it. That's over now, and you don't need to give it another thought. Whatever you've encountered in *the past might make up part of who you are, but it doesn't have to determine where you are going.*

Instead, what we're going to focus on is *a 5-step process for optimizing strategy, creating excellence* in your personal results, and living life with sustainable passion. The beauty of it is that you can apply this strategy not only to your own life, but also to your circle of influence in your professional life. You can use this and teach this in your community and in your work environment.

In fact, the corporate sector is precisely where this process was born - in my decades as a consultant to some of the largest, most successful manufacturing corporations on the planet. Whether it's making pencils, building jet engines, or planning the details of your best life, the process has surprising similarities.

Transformation Step-by-Step

The Advent[5] Process is proven, highly effective and designed to bring you into contact with your deepest self. It evokes transformation through a natural process of *self-definition, self-assertion and self-mastery.* Its results are self-sustaining and life-altering.

Who This Process Is For:

- ◆ Anyone who wants to learn to use a system for effectively and objectively meeting life's challenges while sustaining a heightened level of passion and vitality

- ◆ Anyone who wants to make significant positive changes in life with the easiest, most natural process possible

- Anyone in a position to manage and influence groups brought together for a common purpose
- Anyone who feels they need more direction in life and wants to feel a closer connection to the world around them
- Anyone who has felt blocked from or unworthy of pursuing their deepest Desires
- Anyone who can understand a process and welcomes change

Who It's Not For:

- Anyone who is unwilling to look closely at their key motivations
- Anyone who is addicted to erratic highs and lows fed by drama in their lives
- Anyone who is unwilling to shift their behavior or effect radical change

If you are willing to look at the ideas and concepts of ***Discover the Unseen...*** and the Advent[5] Process, yet don't feel quite ready to make a life change, then keep reading. It might not be the right time for you to transform your life. That's okay! ***We all arrive at our own pace, at the right time and place.*** Perhaps by learning about this process you'll be inspired to take the leap of faith.

I'm confident that you're going to be inspired by what you find ahead. Congratulations on your choice to make this exciting journey of self-discovery. Get ready for a fun ride!

Setting the Stage

Have your heart in your life's work.

— Batten's Wedge

Who am I? - The discovery of my Righteous Cause

My journey of discovery has been alive and with many angles. What I mean is that I have had a sense of awareness and appreciation of all that has been happening in my life which has led me to my Righteous Cause. It all coincides and involves the development and crafting of this book; it shows even in the title. Allow me to share with you how ***Discover the Unseen…*** came to be, and how those events have led me to my Righteous Cause for my life.

The book started out as a business book, with processes and tools to help transform any business to efficiency. I would use the 25-plus years of my experiences and stories of how the processes and tools would lead companies to success. I had spent months outlining and preparing the manuscript for the book and felt good about the coming together of the material. As I have seen and facilitated the processes successfully for many companies in my career, I wanted to share those successes in the book. This all happened prior to my move to another state to finalize the book. Eventually, I moved to Seattle to be close to my publisher, and later the team that is a very important link to the success of this book. However, at the time of the move I was totally unaware of the exciting and unanticipated things that were about to happen in the following 10 months.

The book started out with the basics of how to identify the vision of a company's purpose, then explored the tools and processes necessary to sustain the direction and improvements. I had written over 65,000 words and structured it around a flow, with steps to follow that would assist the reader in achieving the desired results. I had used these processes and tools with leadership teams to set the direction for their company, departments, and employees. One element that was paramount is "ownership," not only from the top management but all the way to the shipping of the product or service to the customer, so it was a holistic approach, getting everyone engaged in the process. Things were coming together and we were pleased with the material; the time had come to edit. However, this is when the shift began, a shift in the direction of the book and/or the message. It seems the book went from a business instructional guide to a book with a message not just for the reader but for my own life.

I was sitting in a restaurant parking lot one afternoon when the transformation showed itself. I had gone to a favorite restaurant I had found in Seattle, a Mexican restaurant that served familiar food much like the TexMex I had grown accustomed to while living in Texas for 25 years. I was just gathering my stuff to go in and have lunch when a presence came over me. It was a presence that was very intimate with me and it filled the car. A voice kept playing in my head over and over again, *"You have to fill the*

void, you have to fill the void, you have to fill the void."This wasn't like a voice you normally hear, but rather one of authority, and it wasn't going away. My body couldn't move from the car. I began to analyze what was happening, thinking it must be my ego at work, but no, this wasn't an ego sounding off, not at all. I sat in the car talking out loud to myself and overcome to tears; the voice wouldn't go away. I am sure the restaurant got reports of a grown man in their parking lot, crying and talking to himself, as many people passed me during this episode.

I asked myself, "What void? What shall I fill it up with?" Then it came to me. It was the book, the book needed to fill the void. "Ok, the book was to fill the void. A business book?" After allowing it to sink in and accepting that something needed to change, it came to me: Ok, ok I will change the book. The book we have must change; we must change the direction of the book with a message. The voice that was so very present and consistent had shifted from "You have to fill the void," to a single message that ***"this isn't big enough."*** So I texted my publisher and told him what had just happened and, being the compassionate professional that he is, he agreed and said we should discuss this new direction.

My publisher and I had not seen each other in some while, so later that week we decided to meet at a downtown Seattle hotel to discuss the book's new direction. We were in the hotel lobby seating area in an open discussion. I kept saying, "It's not big enough," becoming my guiding principle throughout the conversation. My publisher would ask me, "What is it that you want to say to the reader?" and I would respond, "I am not sure, but this isn't big enough." This went on for over three hours.

Finally, in response to what I was sharing from my episode in the parking lot and to the emotions I was exhibiting, he came up with *"It's about your Righteous Cause. The message, your message, is truly about a Righteous Cause."* That was it! I felt a great sense of relief. This was the "void" to be filled. My Righteous Cause was not only to fill my void but many others', and the book was the voice to make that happen. So then, "How could a business book help in finding your Righteous Cause?" became the question to answer.

After brainstorming and mapping out the process, it became clear what was needed and that using the book's existing material was perfect. Let me explain. Companies have a vision and a mission to carry out that vision, and so do you and I. We all have a Desire and a path to fulfill and these ideas, concepts, and processes also apply to an individual just as they do to a company. It made sense; the outline of the business book was the outline for *Discover the Unseen…*

An example from the business world is a story of too much and not everyone understanding the direction. A client had a vision and mission posted on the walls in the office and throughout the company. However, when I would ask random people I would come across in the office and factories, I would hear different interpretations and get some blank stares. This even permeated the operations of the company. I attended a leadership team meeting on financial status. It went on for over two hours with many numbers and figures that were being presented and tossed about. Afterwards, I met with the CEO and asked if that meeting and the information shared had been of value. She said some, but most of it was not useful for her. So

I asked, "What information is valuable; what is the vision you have for the company?" She repeated the same vision that I had seen on the walls and that the figures and numbers were crucial to running the business. After many hours of debating and searching for the real Desire of this leader and company, it came down to, "I want to be profitable and have engaged employees and satisfied customers."

"Now," I said, "that is a vision, a vision that everyone can understand and own."

You see, it wasn't that all those reports were a waste of time because at some point through the years they were necessary. There was a situation that needed a report to understand and ensure that it didn't happen again, but not everyone was aligned with the vision. This was only because the vision wasn't part of the daily activities. Only when everyone in a company understands what it is that the company is about can you look at your individual activities to ensure that everyone is adding value. In this case, with the new vision of "a profitable company with engaged employees and satisfied customers," it was simple to see the alignment or notice when the activities were not productive and consistent throughout the organization.

Much like this example, we, too, have a similar directional malfunction in our Desire. We get caught up in the "foreground" of what we think others want to hear, versus taking the time to look within for the real purpose we want to fulfill. When this is defined, we can build upon this Desire plus align with the process and with what you have, where you are, and what is needed at this current place and time. However, many times for us, as individuals, it's difficult. We must shift from the foreground to viewing from the background to see the unseen, but you will see when you do that it is there, waiting. Just as the CEO did by slowing down and seeking what it was she wanted the company to be, you, too, can do the same.

This can also be a scary process for us, meaning that to find our Desire, the passion of our soul, many times we have to face fear. It doesn't matter who we are, we all have fears that we don't want to face. I believe that *fear and desire live in the exact same space.* In order to discover your Desire, you must face the fear that is blocking you. The CEO had to face the fear of not really knowing why she had all those reports and that she may have to lay off many employees after finding out the reports weren't necessary to run the business, and no one likes to eliminate jobs. We have to face that fear and lean into it with the confidence that we will discover our purpose, our Desire, and our Righteous Cause.

For me it was facing the fear of unworthiness. There was no way that I (Jeff) could ever deliver a message of such importance. I could have stayed the course and ignored the presence that afternoon in the parking lot. But I am so very certain that the dark emptiness would have returned to haunt me once again, as I would not be living out my Righteous Cause. Ever since that afternoon in the parking lot of a Mexican restaurant in Seattle, neither this book nor my life have been the same, and in a very good way. Since we have been following my Righteous Cause, it seems that everyone and everything needed to launch this book and the tour to follow is now falling into place. *These ideas, concepts, and processes are simple but yet so powerful,* and I am excited to be sharing them with each and every one of you!

Who am I? The Advent⁵ Experience.

The purpose of the Advent⁵ Process is to help you get from your current state to your Desired state in the most efficient and sustainable way possible. Your current state is where you are now, and your Desired state is a place of quiet confidence, joy, accomplishment and significance. Even if you don't yet know what your deepest purpose is, the material contained in this book will guide you through the discovery of your innermost Desire and help you build a step-by-step, systematic roadmap to achieve it.

The decades-long development of the Advent⁵ Process began as a result of my natural Desire to continuously improve myself and my comfort with building structured processes. I was at a tough stage in my life, and I knew there were certain techniques I could use to solve a problem and pull myself out of difficult situations. In time, I refined aspects of my ideas, honed techniques, and found myself sharing them with friends, family members and clients.

In the beginning, I didn't have a process, only habit, so I had to create one of my own. I felt the techniques I used to guide companies toward greatness could be translated to lead people toward their Desires. I want to help you avoid the difficulties I went through by giving you *a process that works in just about all situations, every time.* You don't need to come up with this on your own. You can learn from my Adventures and skip the struggles.

Even though I've been using the Advent⁵ Process for years, I see myself on an exciting journey that never ends, and I am still a *co-producer in the design of my own life.* I so relish my work as an author, speaker and coach, and continue to actively manage a consulting business that is thriving. These experiences have all contributed toward the flexibility of this process and it has allowed me to branch into new directions. Using the process has helped me stay connected to my core passions, assemble the resources I need, act on my goals effectively, and achieve a life of joyous fulfillment *even in the face of adversity.*

For me, this is not just a set of good ideas, concepts and processes that I place on the shelf at the end of the day. I live with these principles and apply them in all areas of my life. It's only recently that I've discovered the great need to systematize and share the methods with a wider audience. There are very inspiring times ahead for all of us as we apply ourselves and the message of *Discover the Unseen...*

The *Advent⁵ Process uses symbols* as a visual cue. They provide a mechanism to anchor new ideas and sustain momentum. The five symbols *are Fire, Water, Wind, Sun and Rock.* The number five itself has universal significance in many cultures and ideologies. For example, in China, five is the number of the center, your life path. In numerology, five represents the number of freedom and change. There are five digits on each one of your hands and feet, five senses, and five points on the ancient pyramids.

Advent⁵ is a set of action-driven and results-oriented processes that allow you to participate in the design of your life, with the Elements, a 5-step building process , which helps in defining your Desire, identifying your talents, gathering what's needed to pursue your path, overcoming adversity, and creating a deliberate action plan on a foundation of sustainment. This process will guide you to the element of the one true driving force that each individual has, the one true aim in a person's life.

There is a meaning for your life, one you create with intention. You were created for a purpose and it's just that most of us don't seek it out or look to others for what that purpose could be. *With self-help you seek outside. With Advent⁵ you seek within.*

Harnessing the Elements

Through the first steps in my own life-changing experiences, I was able to craft the early beginnings of this process for identifying and living a life of purpose. It's become my life's work, and I've refined it considerably and continually. I'm thrilled to bring it now to you.

Let's look at a brief overview of the elements in the Advent⁵ Process.

- **Fire:** is useful for providing light and warmth but has the power to consume violently if uncontrolled.

- **Water:** heated water can make steam but must be balanced properly with fire for both to coexist.

- **Wind:** fuels fire and makes it stronger, but left unregulated it can extinguish a weak fire or cause its loss of control.

- **Sun:** is constancy itself, true focus, a deliberate system of naturally unfolding events.

➤ **Rock:** is untouched by fire, water, wind and sun.

1) FIRE: Awareness

Fire is hot and bright. A fire in the hearth or campfire may indicate a peaceful, comfortable, warm center. A rampaging brushfire can symbolize anger and hostility. Fire also symbolizes the metamorphosis of negative energy. *Fire is the eternal flame that inspires you to move. Fire represents your passion, purpose and Desire.*

Fire lets you sort and gain awareness of the past beliefs and negative patterns that have limited you up to this point. It helps you begin to sort through them. It allows you to shake off those limiting beliefs and eliminate non-essentials. You can use the element of Fire *to identify core passions and ignite the Fire of your Desire.*

The first thing we do in this process is take an inventory of activities. We establish a practical set of steps to sort through the elements of your life and remove what's not needed, leaving only what is essential. What remains is the core of our passions. The inner essence is revealed as the outer layers are burned away.

This fundamental step is so simple yet so crucial for leading a life of joy, success and abundance. It means culling the time wasters, shedding the chaff, and embracing the kernel of who we are.

So often what I've seen as people go through this process is the uncovering of an inner light. After taking this step, clients have been able to fully realize their innate talents, understand what drives them, and pursue their true purpose in life. This is the path of destiny, and it reveals the Righteous Cause. The act of pursuing it is the path of bliss, and it ignites the Fire of passion.

2) WATER: Alignment

The element of Water allows for aligning thoughts and actions with the Fire of your Desire. Water helps you select your actions and organize collective wisdom. Water represents the source of abundance. You can use Water to combine the resources – both yours and others' – that are needed to fulfill your Righteous Cause, flowing effortlessly toward the true goal.

Water is a great example of continuous flow and how it always re-adjusts to any obstacles to continue on its path to the end result or destination. Water represents your flow, the path of thought and of collective wisdom. Just as rivers, lakes and oceans carry the parts of many, this force also represents the collective wisdom of many.

Using Water we create a system of flow, tapping from a variety of resources to get the results we're looking for. It means making a plan of action and getting into motion, living in alignment with the Righteous Cause.

This means pulling together resources from a wide-ranging assortment and pooling them together. Using the force of Water, we gather our resources together and create a powerful reserve to draw from. By tapping the diversity around us, we become stronger.

Water reflects what is happening with your emotions.
Water washes and purifies. As water can provide nourishment
to all living things, it can take that same life with floods. Be alert
that the Water doesn't carry you away from your one true aim,
your Righteous Cause.

3) WIND: Adherence

Using the element of Wind means responding to resistance
with renewed commitment. It implies using opposing
momentum for advantage. Wind is about choosing what's
effective and beneficial for your strength, including food you
eat and thoughts you entertain. The force of Wind *allows for
co-creating by your acceptance* of what "is" and making the
choices in alignment with your Desire.

Air provides us energy. A hurricane or strong wind blows
away the artificial and illusory aspects of your life, leaving only
what is fundamentally you. You can push through the problems
in life and become obsessed with distractions, or you can be
pulled by your inner self, and follow your wisdom and your
dreams.

Your inner self is where your Desire lives. Wherever you put
your focus, the energy will follow. "Energy flows where attention
goes." The dreams you have aren't yours by accident. They are
given to you for the purpose of fulfilling them. So *it's your
choice.* Will you take shelter behind the artificial constructs
society bestows upon you, or will you stand firm and confident
upon that which is the essence of you when the Wind inevitably
comes?

Through Advent[5], we learn to lean into the Wind of adversity and embrace the periods of life that create stress, recognizing that the solution to every problem is contained within it. It is about choice and how we choose to respond. This will teach us the way to make healthy choices.

Wind also represents communication with others and yourself, and it signifies the energy of new ideas. It allows us to establish methods for dealing with missteps and adversity while reinforcing our commitment to the process. This means we can establish a standard for continuous improvement.

Just as in boxing or the martial arts, we use the kinetic energy of the forces that oppose us and turn that energy to our advantage. When we do this, we amplify our own personal power. Energy directed toward you is energy you have the choice of using constructively or destructively.

4) SUN: Transforming

The Sun wins the battle against darkness and always rises again. The Sun is the star around which all other celestial bodies of its system revolve. Without the attraction of the Sun, the planets would be mere lifeless objects wandering through the void. So the Sun is the gravitational force that determines the direction and the purpose of the planets. This is also true with us. The Sun will provide the pull, ***the focus and the path of the journey to our Desire.*** It also provides the standardized process for moving forward to the future with a clearly defined present. The Sun represents the centering, focus, direction and alignment of your path.

The element of the Sun is about transforming your routine from a senseless orbit to one aligning your behaviors with your Desire. The Sun means focusing your activities on your Righteous Cause.

It means following a standard path, just as the Sun rises every morning, with predictable changes from season to season. The Sun provides *light to illuminate your path* and the necessary gravity to keep you on it.

With the Sun, we maintain focus on the things that really matter, and we eclipse the ones that don't.

5) ROCK: Foundation

The Rock provides us with a symbol of the certainty of our will. It is also an anchor for the other four of the Advent[5] elements; this provides us the symbol to sustain the renewed alignment with Desire. Rock represents *our strength, commitment and being consistent.*

Rock is solid, but can change form. An earthquake tells you that the foundations of your life are not as secure as you may have thought. From Earth there is new growth, such as mountains, plateaus and vistas.

Rock is strong and resilient. It is able to withstand Fire, Water, Wind and Sun. Rock is your foundation to sustain your Desire, as it is the ownership to make the consistent commitment to do whatever it takes. *The magic of Advent[5] is to transform your Desires with commitment into a rock-solid process of results which you can measure, track and monitor.*

It is about sustaining the process. It means refining choices to keep in alignment with your Desire. We build on a firm foundation that will stand the test of time.

For further explanation and how this process can work for you please visit
www.Advent5.com

Making the "SPACE" for Action

The concepts of Advent⁵ can be applied in all areas of life: Physical, Mental, Emotional, Social and Spiritual. Wherever you find yourself, the process can help you *move from where you are now to where you'd like to be* - even if you don't yet know what that desired destination is.

My life in the corporate sector meant spending a great deal of time in meetings. Anyone who's had the privilege of leading a team of people or championing any team effort knows that meetings go with the territory. In the business world, very little happens without having a meeting first.

Unfortunately, very little seems to happen in meetings at all. Because of this, most people in a position of leadership tend to groan and roll their eyes at the very thought of having another meeting. I used to be one of them.

So often what happens when people come together or when they first begin to pursue an objective is that they fail to plan or to set any kind of intention. This means a great deal of time is wasted determining the purpose and creating the desired outcome. In such cases two or three hours may go by, and in the end everyone is left sitting around wondering what the meeting was about. When it's completed, you ask yourself "what was that about and what am I supposed to do?"

This common theme led me to use an acronym called SPACE. Now no meeting time is ever wasted or mismanaged. Before starting any meeting or launching any new project, we set about to answer a series of questions and work through any issues systematically.

S: Set your intention

P: Purpose

A: Agenda

C: Communicate

E: Expectations

SPACE can be applied in our personal endeavors as well. It will prove to be a useful process to ensure efficiency, alignment and communication.

S: Set Intention – What is the desired outcome of your activity? Write it down. Make a visual and physical representation of what your intention is. In the act of doing so, your idea will become a physical thing, living in the real world. It will move from your mind into reality.

P: Purpose - Why is this important to you and others? Make a note of your desired outcome. Define what this will look like when you're finished with the process.

A: Agenda – Make a checklist of activities with milestones for completion as you move towards your desired outcome.

Schedule time for the activities, and keep track as you complete them.

C: Communicate – Communication is crucial to your success. Communicate with yourself and with others about your process and your desired outcome. Listen, learn and share. Show up with an open mind and a willingness to work. Be ready to have fun, too.

E: Expectations – Identify your expected outcome. Be clear from the start what the end will look like when you get there. Keep it in line with your Righteous Cause.

Points for Review

- ✓ Everyone is born with a higher purpose in life. Not everyone has the knowledge to pursue it. This higher purpose is called your Righteous Cause.
- ✓ Pursuing your Righteous Cause leads to great inner joy and fulfillment. It's what you were born to do.
- ✓ The Advent[5] Process is a process for identifying and pursuing your Righteous Cause. The process uses 5 elements as anchors to easily recall the steps in the system.
- ✓ The Advent[5] Process is highly portable. It can be applied to any problem or pursuit.
- ✓ When you reach a new plateau in your development, you can apply the Advent[5] Process all over again to set and achieve new goals.

Now what.....

Scene 1, we'll discuss fire, the first of the five elements of Advent[5]. We'll take a look at evoking emotions, see where they fit into your personal process, and where you can selectively choose to minimize their effect on your options and behavior.

Living your Righteous Cause through your Desire is the first step. This Desire, which resides within all of us, is the basis of the fire of your passion. Fire is the beginning element of Advent[5], thus leading you on the path to "living on purpose." The Elements are the essence of the book which outlines the process(es) of self-discovery and facilitating the reconnection to what is already there. You can't see it but you know it's there. -TJW

Scene 1
Fire

Defining my Desire - The Point of Origin

Since I'm sharing this process with you, it makes sense to tell you a bit about myself. Knowing where these ideas came from will help you understand how to apply them for yourself. You can use the benefit of my experience to perhaps avoid missteps in your own life.

I'm an educated man, and my work in the corporate sector has brought me success. I'm terrifically pragmatic, using well-defined processes to solve problems; also, I teach and facilitate others to do the same. I'm a person with a highly developed sense of myself and my relationship to the greater world. I'm keenly aware that I'm a spiritual being with a connection to God. Some people are uncomfortable with my saying that, but, frankly, I'm unapologetic about it. I've had to understand this, own it, and fully explore it in order to help the throngs of people who engage me. This concept is not something I can put on and take off like a lab coat, nor would I want to.

My work over the years has helped hundreds of thousands of people, both directly and indirectly. It's richly satisfying work, and the practical process permeates to the core of who we are as people. The elements of the process that have developed enable anyone to *keep the higher view in mind, while providing a practical set of steps for managing a process.*

Everything is a process. We find processes everywhere. From caterpillar to butterfly, nature unfolds moment by moment. As human beings, we're never the same from the moment we're conceived until we take our last breath and beyond. Even as Fire burns, Wind blows and Water flows, the Sun rises and sets, and the Rock maintains its permanent presence - everything is a process.

They say time exists so everything doesn't happen all at once, and space exists so everything doesn't happen to you. Both time and space are factors of process. *Things happen in sequence.* When you get the sequence right, everything flows and life unfolds almost as if by magic. When your fundamentals are flawed, everything falls apart. The bigger the cracks in the foundation, the more flawed the results of the process.

I can say all that now. I know who I am. But it wasn't always this way. Even with the writing of this book, the Advent[5] Process in myself has been, and still is, evolving in each step along this very exciting journey.

Just a Regular Guy

I grew up in America's heartland in a suburb of Kansas City, right on the border between Kansas and Missouri. As in any Midwestern American town, I had as normal an upbringing as you can imagine. I followed a typical story, the story of school, work, marriage and belonging to a family, and I didn't give much thought to the bigger picture.

I attempted to do everything right – that is, everything I was told I was supposed to do. I had everything I was told I was supposed to want. I looked at what others had and began to drive myself in the direction of their dreams. However, at each plateau I felt empty inside, as if all my efforts had been in vain. I kept asking, "Is this all there is?" It was never enough, and I lived with a long list of missed expectations and disappointment. Something felt horribly wrong.

At first there was only a vague sense of uneasiness that thrummed in the back of my brain as I managed the details of my daily life - there was a kind of disconnect from my surroundings. It would rear its face in department meetings once in a while when my mind would momentarily check out and the people I was talking to seemed like strangers. This would also happen in public environments, such as when I was listening to people talk on an airplane. I would think what they were saying was complete nonsense and devoid of value. I'd wonder, *"Who are these crazy people – and what are they doing so close to me?"* I felt critical, completely disconnected, and even alien. The feeling would blink out almost as quickly as it came, and it was hard to identify it.

The feeling would sometimes shadow me as I walked from my car to the curb, or when I'd stand in line at the bank, or when I'd board yet another plane to attend yet another meeting in yet another town.

Then, in time, it became more pervasive. It showed up on the golf course one day and followed me all the way to the 19th hole. It crept in when I'd sit at the dining table with my family over dinner, as if it had pulled up a chair, a sudden and unexpected guest with its own place setting. It appeared to me one morning in the bathroom mirror as I was shaving, and the wall behind me seemed to belong in someone else's story.

It began as a sense of bored dissatisfaction. Quietly it grew into a much deeper threat. There was a hollowness that haunted me. I'd shun the menace as quickly as it tried to assert itself. I couldn't allow it to be real. There was just too much at stake.

Besides the fear of losing everything I had, there was the cultural dynamic of being male. I felt weak and was ashamed that I had feelings like this at all. For me, speaking to someone about the situation would have made it worse. As a man, *I believed I was supposed to be able to solve problems on my own – or better yet, not have them at all!*

My wife and I didn't have a bad marriage. I do remember arguing with her but not so much that it seemed out of line. My now-grown daughter says there was fighting going on, but that kind of dissension is just not part of my memory. I always thought things were manageable enough between us. I was living the life that was given to me, but it had no direction. *I didn't own it.*

What I do know is that after ten years of marriage, most of my life during that time had been spent on the road or submerged in my work. As the hours and days and years racked up, I found I just didn't know my life, and my wife and I were living separate lives. I was more married to my job than to her. In fact, I had fallen out of love with life and I didn't even know it. I found out when it was almost too late.

Dark Night of the Soul

One evening as I drove home from work, I rounded the corner of our suburban block, past the rows of neatly manicured lawns and tightly clipped topiary plantings, and I pressed the button on my remote garage door opener.

The car pulled slowly into the driveway and rolled to a stop, a move I'd practiced thousands of times over the years, so often it was long past being rote.

On this particular night, something was different. This time I wasn't able to bury the disconnected feeling that kept haunting me. Even though I'd been able to shake it off before with a blink or a shift in my thoughts, it had increased its hold rapidly in the past few days. Now it was a shadowy beast looming over the hood of my mid-sized sedan, daring me to get out of the car.

Time slowed, and I began to feel heavy. As the car inched forward, I could feel my will draining from my hands and feet. There was a cold blackness in the pit of my stomach, and my feet seemed to be wearing lead boots. The silk tie around my neck seemed to tighten like a noose, and I could scarcely breathe. My heart pounded, and confusion racked my brain. As the garage door yawned open like a gaping mouth, the cavernous void before me sucked the life out of me. I could not go into my own house.

As I sat staring into the chasm of my garage, counting the neatly stored hand tools mocking me from their pegs, tracing the outline of the incongruous Christmas decorations, rehearsing the fruitless repairs to the lawnmower that I'd need to make yet again during the coming weekend, I felt an inescapable sucking of my soul. The yawning chasm in front of me seemed to be the portal to hell itself.

I couldn't find the words to express even to myself the unbearable hollowness I felt, or the horror at the thought of taking one step farther to go inside and greet my family. I could no longer go on with the charade that my life had become, any more than I could outrun the black feeling that had been shadowing me. It wasn't that I didn't want to go into the house. My being would not allow it. My body would not respond. I sat in the car as time ticked on, staring in a cold sweat and not knowing what to do.

Up to that point I'd done everything right, everything that society told me I was supposed to do. I came from a good family, worked hard at my job, lived in the right neighborhood and had all the right friends, but it was all a lie. *A lie that I became, built upon a foundation of non-authentic self that I had lived for years.* None of it was what I wanted. None of it had anything to do with me. In fact, it was so far away from my essential self that it nearly ended me. It was as if I'd been dropped into someone else's life, and the result was a cruel mockery of all that I am. This was no longer a vague sense of dissatisfaction that nagged at the back of my mind. Now it was a monstrous nightmare that had manifested in front of my car and was robbing me of my will to live.

The emptiness I felt inside on that evening was the stuff of horror novels. *"If I'd had a gun, I would have shot myself."* I just couldn't go on living that lie another moment. In fact, in that moment I felt like I just couldn't go on living.

Even in such instances as these, somehow the mind has a detached reserve of reason. In my case, I was present enough to know that I was in danger, and it scared me to my depths. Up until that point, I'd been living in a state of reaction. For the first time in my adult life, I made a decision.

I backed the car out of the driveway without even going inside to say goodbye, shocked at my own behavior. Somehow deep inside I knew that this wasn't an end but a brave new beginning. I'd won. I was still alive.

Experience has shown that I'm not the first person to feel this way or to endure that sense of disconnection from the source of the living spark. For centuries this experience has been called the "dark night of the soul." It's actually all too common.

However, mine was the first test case for a radical new approach to systematically addressing the cause of this disconnection, reliably infusing life with passion and meaning.

Trial by Fire

When I went through the process of awakening to my situation that day in my car, gazing into the mouth of despair, I knew that I couldn't go on doing the same things in the same way. Just the act of acknowledging that there was a problem released some of the pressure. It allowed me to sit down with my wife and talk about our situation. This was a good thing.

Anyone who's been through a divorce knows that it is a long, drawn-out process, even in the best of circumstances. A marriage is the thorough weaving together of two lives in every respect, and it's meant to be permanent. The completeness and security of marriage is one of the greatest reasons to embrace it. The kind of intimacy that marriage can allow is unmatched.

But when that intimacy fades, when the ***passion no longer burns and the spark of love is gone,*** the bonds that remain are still difficult to disentangle. By weaving together two lives so completely, even a friendly divorce becomes complicated. It's not just an emotional break. It's physical, logistical, financial, familial, social and even spiritual.

The logistics of divorce mean dealing with attachments to household items, real property, investment accounts, insurance, cars, friendships, extended family, community involvement and every other area of daily life that you and your spouse have enjoyed together.

The sorting process that happens naturally in a divorce completely transforms the status quo. The person you've been calling mother and father, even with the words "in-law" attached, may choose to stop talking to you, no matter how close you may have been in the past. The relationship may just fade out, or it may be extinguished all at once. On the other hand, your spouse's family may continue to embrace you as their own.

While such a radical shift in lifestyle often leads to new devices and can lead to a state of depression, it doesn't have to be this way. *Perception is a choice,* and in my case this sweeping change was both fearsome and freeing. I'd feared breaking the news to my daughter about leaving her mother, and at the same time it was truly liberating at a deep level. She had seen it coming for a long time.

Many radical shifts in life offer the same kind of dread and relief. A move to another town, going back to school, taking up a banner for a worthy cause, or even the simple act of welcoming a new pet or family member into the household can throw off the balance of daily life and make procrastination a welcome option.

I was really relieved that my daughter had taken the news so well. In the face of her calm acceptance, it gave me permission to focus on my own need to move on, to take the next steps and build a new life. The result was a division of property and a letting go of the things that weren't working for my wife and me.

The Letting go of so many entanglements allowed me to start fresh. It meant I could choose. It meant I could decide my course based on my passions, my self-knowledge and my desires for the future. It meant I could live a life of joy and fulfillment without tripping over past mistakes. The break-up of my marriage took all the power out of the choices I'd made in the past that had been motivated by peer pressure. In many ways, I had a clean slate.

The number one goal of the subconscious mind is to keep you safe and alive. *In most cases, the subconscious believes that change is dangerous.* Your brain will do everything possible to keep things the same, even if those things aren't good for you. While my life was in the process of a re-design, I felt a deep-seated need for a certain amount of continuity. It's only natural. In fact, it's very human.

What I didn't realize at the time of my divorce was that suddenly having a clean slate also meant a sudden and desperate unconscious need for me to hold onto whatever else was working for me at the time, even if it was working only in a marginal way. Because I was going through a divorce, I unconsciously tried to **hold onto the status quo, including the things that were making me feel disconnected.** I began to bury this nightmare, just as I'd done with many of the others in my life, and pretended everything was all right. In some ways I continued to live in reaction to my surroundings. I wasn't yet comfortable with the concept that I could choose at all. **Choosing was a habit I hadn't yet gotten accustomed to.**

Changing careers in the middle of a divorce didn't occur to me as an option. It was enough that I was dealing with my dissatisfaction at home. The career change could wait, I thought at the time. Deep down, I knew more change was coming.

When my wife and I split, it seemed natural for me to move to Texas. My job required me to be there quite a bit, and the move was facilitated by our divorce. I thought the change of cities would do me good and fuel the spark of passion once more in my life. It seemed like a good move for me to make at the time. Just what the doctor ordered – a fresh start in a new town.

It was a very tough choice to make because I didn't want to leave my daughter behind. Not long afterward, she came to visit me for the summer and wound up staying with me through high school. Once again, **the thing that I'd been dreading turned**

out to be something I should have gladly embraced. If I hadn't moved away, all kinds of wonderful experiences would have been denied me and my daughter.

In time, the feeling of growing dissatisfaction in my work began to show itself again. It was growing in the same way as it had before. That dark feeling was becoming just as forceful as it had been that day I sat in my car back in Kansas City, staring into the abyss of my suburban garage. This time, though, its face was familiar and I knew how menacing it could be. I had the benefit of hindsight, and I had the wisdom to not suppress but confront those feelings.

After a few years of slogging through my daily routine, it became clear that the time had come to change careers. The stress of my work was reaching a critical point, and I knew I couldn't keep spending my days in pursuit of nothing but money and power. My work had to have some kind of meaning.

Enter another distraction and an opportunity to bury the "darkness of the soul." I started living in the fast lane, going to the local bars/restaurants for happy hours, dating, playing golf, attending many business associations and dinner clubs. With the dissatisfaction of my career in Texas, I decided to quit my job without any prospects or even an idea of what I would do. I was still looking on the outside, the foreground, for something or someone to fill the emptiness that continued to haunt me.

On a subconscious level, I knew I needed to pursue my passion, my Desire. Consciously, I was only looking for a change of pace, some new hobby to occupy my time. Without realizing it, I'd already made the decision to pursue a different career, something that would help people and make a difference in their lives. This decision made itself apparent to me in a subtle way, as a quiet hint whispered to the back of my mind one day at the local library. ***Great storms announce themselves with a simple breeze.***

Even with my marriage ended and the move for my job already behind me, I knew my process wasn't complete. It was merely underway. Even though I wasn't through the depths of my soul's dark struggle, I was in motion and heading in the right direction. I was sure the right move would reveal itself. It was only a matter of time before this step in the process would become apparent.

What I arrived at through this experience is the human need to spend less time on how much we know and ***spend more time sparking the imagination.*** In this process, I knew that some things in my life weren't working. ***I sorted through the pieces of my life and identified what to keep, what to discard.***

Fire has a transmuting effect as it takes wood and transmutes it to a flame. We, too, have the ability to transform our inner flame – our Desire - into energy to transmute those inner desires into advancement on our journey.

Forget that imagination is something many of us have been taught to suppress and explore what your inner being is telling you. ***Shake off those limiting beliefs and clear space for the Fire of your Desire.***

The Answers are Already Here

At the center of your being you have the answer; you know who you are and you know what you want.

— Lao Tzu

You can spend a year traveling the world to explore religions or spend years studying all of the different philosophies in search of the holy grail. Or you can take but one small journey into your soul to understand the nature of yourself. The answers are already inside you. It's a matter of letting them come to the surface.

In the quotation above, Lao Tzu offers a very profound idea, and on the way or the path to the discovery of YOU this sometimes means letting go - letting go of the past, future, toxic relationships with people and things, limiting beliefs, false identities, daily distractions, and thoughts that add no value to your daily life. These are all "form" that enter your space, and you have a choice either to react or respond. *It's your choice.* This is a powerful idea, and you can use it to bring about radical change in your life.

As you clear the space in the present moment, you become aware of the form and your relationship with it. Your Desire comes from your authentic self, and it will become clear as you sort out the things you don't desire. With that clarity comes happiness.

If we are going to spend our time interacting with all that is here, shouldn't we choose to use that time doing what gives us strength, confidence, happiness, and love? It only makes sense to use the time we're given in this life for the things that matter most.

The truth is that **all the answers you seek are not in the world outside, but in the world within.** The outside world will provide you with what you need if only you ask for it. First you must find your meaning, your purpose and Desire.

The Advent⁵ Elements - Fire that Burns Within

You already know what your deepest Desire is. It burns inside you like a flame. However, whether or not you're consciously aware of it is another matter. Your inner flame may be covered up with a lot of extra things, things that don't mean as much to you as your core passion. This clutter in your consciousness may be preventing you from seeing what's deeply important. That doesn't mean your passion isn't there; it's just not the focus or the path of your mind.

We've said that the Advent⁵ Process maps to five elements.

The first element is *Fire, the flame of passion*. This means the *first phase is a sorting process,* removing the "dead wood" from life and transforming your decision-making with the fire of your passion. What remains is the precious gift at the core of your individuality, your reason for being. Using this passion – this gift or talent – becomes *your life's Righteous Cause.*

Your Righteous Cause is at the core of your motivation from the time you wake up until the time you go to sleep. If you're not consciously aware of it, life's activities seem to be random and the motion of life itself seems rudderless. You drift from one thing to another, moving through your daily activities in an empty state of sleep-walking. Your work lacks that spark of life, and your off-hours are unfulfilling. You feel neither hot nor cold, and your days have neither highs nor lows. ***With the acceptance and engagement of your Righteous Cause you're in the flow, the flow of being truly alive.***

Areas for Self-Assessment

Take a moment now to look at these aspects of your character and do a little bit of self-assessment. Give some real thought to your answers. They may surprise you.

Your Interests - The activities you like to do may offer you clues about career or occupational interests, or even life pursuits you hadn't thought of before.

Your Personality - Everyone's unique combination of emotions and psychology make up their personality. What does your personality look like? Keep your answer to 25 words or less.

Your Skills - Skills are developed from past experiences as well as from community involvement and other roles you play in life. Do you volunteer for a favorite cause? Do other families count on you to fill a central role? Are you someone people often seek out for advice? Weigh your answers carefully.

Your Abilities - Talents and inborn abilities often indicate your untapped potential. Sometimes people take for granted the skills that come easily. Ironically, those are exactly the areas that you ought to explore. Identifying your core passions and aligning them with your innate abilities is the best possible combination. With training, natural aptitudes can easily turn into options for life pursuits.

Your Values – Values are the guidelines of what you hold close to your heart, the situations where you make a stand for something. The personal motivation for career and life satisfaction is different for everyone. By taking a look at your values, you can prioritize the role that your career plays in your life. In the course of time, your values might shift a bit. Something you strongly believe at age twenty may not match your values at age forty or fifty.

Values represent a key element in defining our desire and our journey. We all say we're clear about them, but at times the distinctions can become blurred. To move to the next level we have to be clear on what we value. Values are a means of communicating to ourselves what we consider worthy, excellent, useful or important.

Your Beliefs - Beliefs are the assumptions we make about ourselves, about others in the world, and about how we expect things to be. Beliefs represent how we think things really are, what we think is really true, and what we therefore expect as likely consequences that will follow from our behavior. The clearer you are about what *you value and believe in,* the happier and more effective you will be.

Your Lifestyle and Finances - Your preferred living conditions can impact your career and occupational choices, and vice versa. By *evaluating your lifestyle* and the finances you need to support it, you can examine your decisions about your life pursuits. You can also see clearly how these decisions may affect you and your family. Financial needs are an important factor in the choices you make about how you spend your time.

Your Surroundings - Conditions in your daily life may be just as important as how you decide to spend your time, whether it's working, studying, volunteering or leisure time. Your work *environment may play a big part in how you feel* about your job or daily activities. The reality is that your comfort level with where you are may make all the difference in the success of how you spend your time.

Defining Your Desire

Think back to a time when you were really happy about something you had done or participated in, an activity that brought you joy or fulfillment. Now think ahead to something you dream of doing, and imagine how that would make you feel. Borrow the emotion from your past successes to envision your successful future.

Listen to yourself. What types of activities bring you happiness? Here are some exercises to help you define your Desire.

Who I Am – In this exercise, *detach from distractions of the foreground and go within.* Take ten minutes to quiet your mind. You may focus your gaze on a candle flame during this time, or you may choose to close your eyes and focus on your breath. The purpose is to go to the stillness of your authentic self and focus on one thing such as the candle flame and allow all other thoughts and distractions to pass by – meaning, don't identify with them, just observe them from the background.

During this period when your mind is quiet, ask yourself "Who am I?" We are looking for your inner self, the self that is always there and never leaves but not the self you identify with such as I am a truck driver, I am a mother, father, family member, I am part of the country club, school, business – the question is, "Who am I?" Let each word drift back to the origin of thought (the stillness), the space of the inner voice. You don't need to force an answer. Just be aware of the thought, ponder the question, and be open to receiving the answer. It will surface at that moment or perhaps at a later time, but it will surface at the right time.

Inner Essence – In this exercise, make a list of the things you're attracted to doing. Brainstorm the things you're good at as well as the things you love to do. What do others say you are good at? What comes naturally to you? What do you enjoy doing? *What leaves you feeling happy and fulfilled?*

Talents – Now make a list of what excites you. What are those things you love doing when you are using your God-given talents? Ask yourself what it is that you want. What would make you happy? Who do you want to hang around? Make note of the type of environment you want to occupy. Write down the people you look up to. What lifestyle do you dream of? *How can I use my talents to align with the very things that excite me?*

Mapping Your Dreams - What are some of your best dreams? Write your talents and dreams on a single page. Select the ones that are in *alignment with who you are*, what you are good at, and what gives you the most satisfaction. Take time to review and rearrange them, and see what *pattern feels right for you.*

Defining the Details - Outline your desire. Use the pattern from the dream mapping to define what makes you excited. Given your talents and dreams, what would *inspire the most passion for you?* Imagine you have everything you need to fulfill this desire. Create a picture and visualize in your mind what this looks and feels like.

Alignment - Complete these sentences based on your innermost desire.

1. My intention is…
2. My visual is…
3. My feelings are…
4. My actions are…
5. My commitment is…

It All Becomes Clear

When you have identified your true core passion, it shines like a light in the back of your eyes. It's as if the Sun lives in your heart. The nagging questions that used to plague you are nowhere to be found, your movement begins to flow and collect as Water in a river, and it's as if the Wind of *resistance is calmed by your certainty.* It all seems so clear. Life seems to flow effortlessly like a running stream, and any apparent set-backs are quickly overcome. Your days endure like they're on a Rock solid foundation, and the course is clear. You eagerly arise out of bed with the Fire of passion pulsing through your veins and can hardly wait to see what happens next and actively participate in your Desire. It becomes so simple, almost magical, as if you are *living on your intended purpose* and it is all making sense.

However, at this point you may begin to feel bogged down by too many thoughts, a sort of chatter in your mind. Do they just show up for no apparent reason? *You're not alone.* This is happening to many people in today's frantic society. There are so many distractions and so much information bombarding us at every single moment. The key is to quiet the mind. Be aware of that space, the space you know is there but may fear. Then you will begin to identify the distractions.

To address this, you can do some writing using a pen and paper. There's something about the physical act of *translating a thought through the physical effort* of writing that locks it into your sense memory. Writing involves more hand-eye coordination than typing does. It also requires you to slow down and ponder the meaning of what you're saying. Here is a simple three-step process that will guide you.

Step 1

Make a list of the thoughts you have. Don't think about them; just write them down. At the end of the day before you go to bed, take the list and organize your thoughts. Try to categorize them into some kind of flow. For many people who do this exercise, most of these thoughts are worries, negative by nature. This is completely normal but by no means is it desirable. The good news is you can *choose the thoughts you wish to think about.* However, first you need to understand them. Be the observer of your thoughts. Ask yourself questions about these thoughts, such as "Where did that one come from?" and "How does this make me feel?" Don't over-analyze them. Just write down the first answer that comes to you.

Step 2

Before you go to sleep, *set your intention* either verbally or by writing it down. I suggest writing it down in your Advent[5] journal so we can review it at a later time. Choose to learn while you sleep and let your subconscious mind give you the answers. Ask God through your thoughts and prayers to enlighten you about all the thoughts you are having. Ask which ones you should assign action to.

Step 3

Now imagine how it will feel to be at peace with all those thoughts – think from the end. Give this a chance tonight and for the next week. Keep a journal of your progress. At the end of that time, review your progress. You'll be amazed at how much change you see in just one week. Relax and be happy, knowing *you are in the right place.* You are exactly where you are supposed to be.

Limiting Beliefs – These create a negative world of energy that attracts more of the same. The world mirrors the energy you send out and allows the abundance of that energy to flow to you. That being said, the limiting beliefs you hold within you become amplified through a continual negative feedback loop. *The more you think poorly of yourself, the more your environment reinforces that message for you.*

What you believe is what your reality becomes. Be aware of negative self-talk, limiting beliefs and small thinking, and recognize it for what it is. There's no need to criticize yourself if you catch yourself in negativity. Simply make the choice to observe your pattern of thought as it is.

When you catch yourself in a limiting belief, ask yourself whether you truly feel that way. Is it true, is it absolutely true? Get to the core of the emotion, and then ask yourself if feeling that way is serving you. If it isn't, ask yourself when you will be willing to let it go. Wait for the answer; it will most likely come immediately. You have the power to transform the thought for your higher good. You have the power to change your habits of mind. *It all starts with awareness.*

A Sense of Meaning and Purpose

Those who have succeeded in achieving their dreams will tell you that the journey on the path to their Desire was thrilling and joyful. They will often tell you, "I've dreamed of this since I was a child. I imagined it, I pretended it, and I used to practice as if I were really doing it."

I have the honor of living out my passion by sharing these ideas, concepts and processes with a wider audience. All I had to do was uncover what was discouraged in my adult years. For me it meant embracing my imagination and using it to help people. *The epiphany is that the gift was always there;* it was just covered up by the daily distractions and old limiting beliefs.

Your truth is the alignment of energy and the power of momentum. *It doesn't matter what anybody else thinks about your Desire. It only matters what you think about it.* This truth is pure and free of judgment.

So I would challenge you to ask yourself a couple of questions. What is it that you imagine? Has it been absent in your life? Enter them in your journal and let's see how they influence your patterns, how they align with your Desire.

Maybe you already have the things you need, the things you've been told to desire - a comfortable home, good food, a loving family, a steady job and plenty of friends. Even so, a nagging emptiness may haunt you. Clouds of doubt may trouble you in your seemingly perfect life. *What could be the cause? What could be missing from your life?*

One of the greatest benefits you can get from identifying your core passion and flowing consciously, *deliberately on your Righteous Cause* is a sense of meaning and purpose in your life. This uplifting inspiration will consume any depressing thoughts or low self-esteem you might otherwise feel. You will be fired up by your own deeds and thoughts as you go about your daily life.

To *live an inspired life* is to walk with an enhanced awareness of everyone and everything around you, to see divinity and delight in everyday people and events, and to infuse your environment with the same magical energy. That may sound mystical and out of reach. However, living an inspired life can be practiced daily by connecting with the Fire of your core passion - your Desire.

We are constantly being engaged by our five senses. Immerse your senses in reading, listening, talking, touching and breathing in the experiences that support your Righteous Cause, aligned with your Desire.

Here is a look at some qualities that are the hallmarks of an inspired life and how they might relate to your core passion.

Honesty and Conviction – Acting with integrity, this being the act of wholeness. *Be yourself and believe in yourself.* Ask for what you want and express yourself clearly. Seek the truth, and follow only what you believe is in alignment with it. As you do, the details of your life will become uncomplicated and filled with profound peace.

Love and Compassion – Dedicate a portion of your time and attention to people who don't have the advantages you do. Act with kindness toward others, friends, family and strangers alike. Do your work passionately until you find your true vocation, where loving your work comes naturally. Also, be in a state of appreciation for all that is and all that you are – *love all that is every part of you and all you encounter.*

Courage – Declare your greatest dreams as your intention. *Embrace your deepest fears and lean into the adversity with confidence.* Persevere and be consistent, even when the going gets rough.

As you embrace these qualities, it's also important to maintain a sense of efficiency. ***Dream of the future, but live in the present.*** You can quiet the distractions in your mind by staying close to the Fire of your conviction. Let your Desire prepare you to build the foundation under your dreams with honesty, love and courage.

Our main objective in working with Fire is to peel back the layers of your activity, reduce the many areas of your focus, and identify your core passions. This process sets the stage for a total transformation of your business and personal life. You can ***achieve outstanding results and create an atmosphere of total simplicity*** in your personal environment. Remove the unnecessary situations, tasks and objects from your life, leaving your passions, your motivations, and those things already in your life that are worth keeping.

It seems so simple, yet ***most things that really matter are simple.*** It's when we identify with the distractions that things become complicated. It's our choice. This concept can be applied in any number of ways. Keeping things simple and uncomplicated allows us to see our Fire and the path of our Desire.

This process began in the corporate world, but you'll begin to see how beautifully these steps apply equally to areas where problems arise and need to be solved, and in addressing that emptiness you may feel inside. You'll see how this relates to managing the practical details of everyday life, as well as ***setting yourself on a path of self-discovery and fulfillment.***

Passion Tempered with Logic

You can use the Advent[5] Process to identify your core passion, and at the same time use it to remove emotions from your decision-making process. The fundamental application is about problem solving awareness using rational, deliberate methods.

In this space, *Fire represents your passion, purpose and Desire.* Fire that is hot and bright serves a dual purpose. A fire in the hearth may offer a peaceful, comfortable, warm center. It's the heart of the home, a place where people congregate for food, light, life-giving warmth and conversation. In this case, you can use Fire purposefully as a force for good. It transmutes negative energy into positive results.

However, Fire can easily be a force for destruction. A wildfire can wipe out anything in its path and bring devastation where it's not contained.

The Fire of passion has the same properties. Passion can be a force for good, fueling you to acts of brilliance and even heroism. But unharnessed passion can rapidly explode into anger and hostility, harming all those affected by it. Temper your passion with reason.

Intention Sets the Direction

Now that you have your Desire defined, you need to set your direction. In fact, defining your direction is crucial for your success in creating results fueled by your deepest desires. To get the results you want, you need to set an intention. *An intention is a deliberate action, in alignment with your Fire.*

It's easy to become inactive at times because we spend so much time trying to figure out how we are going to do something. When that happens, momentum gets stalled. Another obstacle is the belief that it can't be done because the path doesn't seem clear. *The confused mind does nothing, so here again progress can be stalled.*

Use your innate talents to pursue the objectives that you know you can achieve and that have inherent appeal for you. Take what you have in the current situation and use it, starting at this point in time – right now. *Identify the talents you don't possess with an intention of seeking those who do.*

Results mean everything. Results are your method of ensuring that your direction is on the path toward your Desire. Focusing on the ideas of Fire will allow you to get the results that are in line with your aims.

If you attempt something and it doesn't work, it only means that you've identified one way not to reach your desired outcome. Now that you've eliminated that possibility, you can take the lessons learned from this attempt and use them in your next step in the process. *There are no failures, only results.* Allow and accept the feedback with an open mind, with no emotions attached, and move on.

Apply the principles of Fire to determine what it is that you really want, where you want to be, determine what you need to do to get there, and discover how to apply the steps within Fire to build the foundation of your Desire.

You can apply the Advent[5] Fire process to a variety of areas, including life assessment, energy attachments, and your

Righteous Cause. *Sort through all you have and align what is needed to fulfill your Righteous Cause.*

Applying Fire as a life assessment tool means taking a look at the logistics of your life to determine what works, what doesn't, and what to focus on. By identifying what to keep and what to eliminate, the complete mechanism of your life begins to build momentum on its own. Suddenly, the things that held you back are no longer the focus of your attention. The result is that you can *see clearly what matters most* and always keep it in view.

Identifying what increases your energy and what drains it is critical in your life assessment. Take a look at how you spend your time, the activities that consume most of your attention, the food you consume and the feelings that you have toward those activities.

Let's say that you own a company and most of your time is being spent performing accounting tasks. If you're not drawn to accounting type activities, you're likely to find this a terribly dull effort and a waste of your valuable time. It's likely to drain you of your precious energy and drive. If you're like most people, the lackluster feeling you cultivate when you spend time in this space can spread into other areas of your personal and professional life. Odds are that your business isn't doing well if the majority of your focus is on the accounting instead of spending that vital energy on using your innate talents.

When you're in the zone – when you're using your talents and you're pursuing the path of your Righteous Cause, there is no limit to your energy. You could go all day and night, skip meals, forego sleep and still feel fresh and alive. When you pursue the Fire of your Desire, you are living as you were intended to live.

Here are a few questions that will reaffirm your Desire. What is it that keeps you up at night? What makes you wake up early and bound out of bed with a smile on your face? How can you bring this joy to others? This is your life's purpose – the source of your talent, and the beacon that draws you forward and inward. Your passion will drive you to your purpose.

Use these ideas, concepts and processes of Advent⁵ to examine the core of *your passions and identify your Righteous Cause.*

Sparking the Fire of Your Desire

Defining what you want seems to be the biggest question facing most people. If you never cultivate your creative side, you may never find out its full potential. Most people feel extreme pressure their whole lives about how to look, what to say, how to behave, whom to like, what to like and where to be. Society doesn't usually promote creativity or encourage looking inside to find that one true desire.

Ironically, the same is true for your logical side. If you're profoundly creative and you don't develop your sense of logic to its full potential, you won't know what you're capable of. This issue isn't as common, but it does occur.

The balance factor is a huge contributor to the way our lives turn out and the choices we make. The bottom line is that we are seldom taught to seek our God-given talents, those things we are good at and enjoy doing. Typically, we are subject to the structure of the classroom, and we're taught to complete all our assigned homework in order to understand the lessons. But I would suggest that we're not given the right lessons to learn, and the lessons we're given are drummed into us by routine instead of allowing us to learn by experience.

Our level of confidence in our ability to achieve our desires serves as a governor over our choices. Many people don't believe in their ability to reach their goals, or perhaps more commonly, *they don't believe in their own worthiness* to attain them. Others place their faith in the wrong people to assist them, lending too much power or confidence to those unqualified to help them achieve their aims. Looking outside oneself for confidence and worthiness is an exercise in futility. You're looking in the wrong direction.

This kind of personal history can inhibit our choices, even cause us to turn a blind eye to our true desires. This is also true when we are distracted by the day-to-day living situations we all encounter.

Once you have identified those things that interfere with and distract from the Creative Source, you will be more likely to find the places and the energy that match your Desire. You can and will make more effective choices about your thoughts, environment, and the people you associate with.

Communicate with yourself as if you have achieved what it is that you desire. This is not to say that you can delude yourself into believing that you have already achieved your Desire. It is to have a sense of outward and inward belief plus the confidence that the very thing you desire is true and will come true. This will help you with the actions. Have a sense of urgency and develop an awareness of the present moment. The time is now, your time is now. *Now is all we can act on, so have the sense of urgency that will move you now.*

Take the time to really understand your passions and do the research. As a society, we spend so much of our time pleasing others, attempting to be someone other than ourselves, doing what is expected of us or doing what we think we should do. These will quench the Fire.

Be cautious of being *caught up in the illusion of compliance.* Don't be lulled into a false sense of security by staying in a space or the same place, remaining in a situation that is comfortable, even if that situation doesn't benefit you. It may even be hurting you. Many times we stay with a known quantity because it is familiar and even comfortable. We have become accustomed to this place where we are not surprised and know what to expect. However, if it is not in alignment with a greater dream, we risk becoming complacent and prevent movement onto what it is we truly desire.

You are in alignment with God and your role in the universe when you are in that blissful state of mind. In other words, you are doing what you were meant to do. When you pursue your life's purpose, your life becomes a constant state of joy. *You are living out the journey as you were intended.*

Perhaps this is a good time to define some important terms as they relate to this book and the Advent[5] Process.

Desire: A desire is a deep-rooted purpose in your soul. It is the essence of who you are. A desire gives you passion, direction and will.

Dream: A dream can be an object, a place, a person or a thing. A dream is something we wish for and many times can give us deep satisfaction. A dream is thought of as perhaps someday being fulfilled.

Goal: A goal is a dream with a deadline attached to it.

Both dreams and desires are innate and are given to you by God. They can be determined by you and only by you. Goals can be imposed on you by others, but wherever they originate, most often they're only achieved through deliberate action.

Combining a dream and a desire can be a powerful tool. Take a moment now for this exercise. List both and see how they can be aligned to achieve your ultimate Desire. What do you want? Write down what attracted you to this process.

Desires:

🍂

🍂

Dreams:

🍂

🍂

Harmonious Abundance: The Real Goal

Harmonious abundance means being free to do what we want when we want to do it most of the time. It means having plenty in an effortless way. It means *freedom from self-generated stress.* We all have the need to work, but what if the work is a labor of love and not a burden? Harmonious abundance means being certain that your income goals are met predictably and consistently. Keep in mind, as we have discussed before, that accepting what is means all that comes in your path is useful in some way. It's not the elimination of any situation or issue but how you respond that is part of the goal journey.

The goal is to live a good life and have nice things without engaging in the distractions and downsides inherent to any situation.

How Do We Get There?

Your blueprint for harmonious abundance will change all the time, and it comes with a lifestyle change. A good starting point is to cover the essentials and get a life upgrade.

Instead of focusing on the mountain, focus on the milestones. Only *focus on the present moment* and what is at hand, neither anticipating tomorrow nor analyzing what happened in the past.

Why This Works:

When you break it down, it manages the emotion of being overwhelmed. Feeling overwhelmed is the biggest hindrance that most people encounter. *Map out the starting and ending points using the map.* Draw a line between them and mark the milestones. Focus on the core milestones, and work through the steps. Keep it simple, using what you have at this given moment to move forward. Take stock of the assets included in the current situation, and make the most of them.

Recap and Next Steps

At this point, you have defined your Desire, Dream and Talents – congratulations! Now we need to organize, align and ***build a new process that you create*** that allows you to move forward and propels you in the direction of your vision. Let's look at a process that might help. We've used the concept in many businesses worldwide, and even with individuals, with great success.

The Advent[5] Process maps to five elements, and we've just discussed the first one, Fire, the flame of passion. Here is a review of that element and how you can apply it in your quest.

Fire, the first phase, is a sorting process, removing the "dead wood" from life and transforming your decision-making with the Fire of your passion. What remains is the precious gift at the core of your individuality, your reason for being. Using this ***passion – this gift or talent – becomes your life's Righteous Cause.***

Your Righteous Cause is at the core of your motivation from the time you wake up until the time you go to sleep. You already know what your deepest desire is. It burns inside you like a flame. Right now it may be covered up with things that don't mean as much to you as your core passion. This clutter in your consciousness may be preventing you from seeing what's deeply important. That doesn't mean your passion isn't there; you're just not fully aware of it.

Use the energy of Fire to remove whatever is covering up your core passion to sift through your thoughts, emotions and limiting beliefs, to define or discover the ones that are aligned with your Desire. Actively participate with this process and the Fire of your passion will burn in your eyes as if you are lit from within. After all, *you are this Fire,* it comes directly from you and it's always been there.

It is paramount that you have defined, discovered, and uncovered your true Desire. If you have not, you will end up with a distorted path that will bring frustration and lack of faith in yourself. Earlier we discussed the point of a sense of urgency; however, taking the time to ensure you are beginning the journey with your authentic self identified will ensure success. Slow never fails to arrive. Being in tune with your rhythm and not the rhythm of the "foreground" is critical.

Forever has only just begun. In this time and space, time seems to warrant a sense of urgency. However, in the big scheme of things….we have just begun, proving once again that time is always on your side. So there is no need to worry, no need to fret. If we align with our Desire (the messenger of your Soul), *the elements of the Advent⁵ Process plus faith in yourself and God,* you will realize that you are exactly where you need to be at the right time!

Water

The Collection and Getting Into Action

I knew that I was ready for a change, and though I'd decided to make a professional shift, it was long in coming. Maybe it was the fact that I'd been through a big life change and I wasn't ready to make a career change at the same time. Perhaps it was the fact that the longer you put something off, the bigger the task becomes in your mind. I think it was a bit of both in this case, and I didn't act on my deep desires for some time. In fact, it was years. Sometimes I think on those years now and I wonder what I was waiting for, but I've come to know that no experience is wasted. ***Everything happens for a reason.*** We have the responsibility to look past the foreground and look for what is present – what the message is.

A lot happened in that time, quitting my corporate job, a new intimate relationship, and another opportunity that was given to me. A friend in California had asked me to help his company refine their manufacturing process, and it seemed to him that I was the perfect candidate for the job. The problem was that I didn't want a job at all. After more than a decade of working for the other guy, I was burned out and fed up with the corporate environment. Though I admired my friend and appreciated the opportunity he was offering me, I just couldn't bring myself to say yes.

"Then we'll hire you on as a consultant," he said, and in a moment, my future had been decided for me. I accepted as a reaction to the offer; it still wasn't my choice. Nonetheless, it was an opportunity, and a better one than anything else I had in the works at the time.

I named my business and hung a sign on the door. I was still in Texas, still working in the same industry, but now I had greater autonomy and I selected the clients and jobs I would service. For the moment, I was excited.

Still, the fact remained that I was doing the same type of work that I had been doing before. The names of the companies had changed, the faces were different, and yet there was still something missing. Once again, I hadn't chosen; I'd accepted what was given to me, and I made the most of it. Don't misunderstand me, I enjoyed, and was grateful for, my new career as a consultant and it was rewarding for the companies, employees and even myself. We were making changes and facilitating meaningful and beneficial transformation. However I did not own the decision to move in that direction. The opportunity was given to me but something was still missing.

This is a key point: *unless you choose, the choice will be made for you.* Life will give you whatever is left over after serving those who are decisive.

I was living in Houston by this time. My daughter had grown up and gone off to college and I had just gone through the process of ending an intimate relationship that didn't work out.

I was truly on my own, with nothing remarkable to show in my own life for the passage of time, except for the stuff accumulated by living a lie in pursuit of someone else's dream.

It was at this point that a good friend of mine suffered a sudden loss. She needed help emotionally and logistically to deal with a sudden death in her family, and I temporarily moved to the nearby small town where she lived. I knew I was helping her through a tough time, which offered some kind of satisfaction. Dedicating myself to assisting her didn't leave me a lot of time for me to focus on what it was that I wanted, though. While it was clear she was at a point of transition, I, too, was taking a pause and planning my next move. Once again I was without an intimate partner and stuck in a fog of pain and emptiness.

I still had my consulting business, which, for the most part, was running itself. I had set it up as a business rather than as a self-employment model. The people I'd hired to run the company were doing fine without me. I could step into and out of the flow of business without a great deal of hassle. The work was rewarding, but I wanted something more. It was great to help people solve their problems. To me, the problems we were helping them solve didn't matter enough to me. *I still saw the world through half-lidded eyes – bored, distracted, feeling like an outsider.*

My friend's sudden loss reminded me of the brevity of life. I don't fear death, but I knew I wasn't making the most of the life I'd been given. I was finally ready to make that career change. I wasn't at all clear on what that looked like, but I knew I wasn't happy and not living my Desire. At the time I didn't even know what my Desire was, but I had *the sinking feeling that this wasn't it.*

One evening that summer I went to the library as an escape, and I found myself searching online. I was looking for some kind of solace, some piece of information that would shift my state, both emotionally and mentally. I didn't have anything concrete in mind, but I knew that I wanted to help people – to find an activity that would keep the focus on serving others. That much was sure. As much as I'd been able to lend my strength to my friend in her tough time, my soul had responded with a kind of resiliency I didn't really know I had. I caught a glimpse of something greater in the world outside myself, and it suited me to be of service. I knew that's what I wanted, I felt compelled to do so. This feeling seemed to come from within and I wasn't certain where it was coming from.

There, at the library, I stumbled upon some job postings online. I saw an ad for a sales position at a Dallas motivational corporation, a personal development company, and suddenly I just knew that this was what I was looking for.

As a young professional, I'd been a great fan of self-help motivational books and their processes. This company has been at the peak of the personal development industry for a very long time. I knew if I could get involved with them, I would be able to help not just one person at a time but hundreds of thousands, perhaps even millions of people. *My work wouldn't just be a job, it would be a calling.* A calling in a more one-on-one interaction on a more personal level than the consulting business had provided thus far.

All of this played out in my mind as I sat there at the computer in the library that night, surrounded by nameless strangers. I was so excited, I wanted to grab the people around me and tell them all about the new job I'd found. By pooling my resources, I'd finally found the means to align myself with the Fire of my Desire. I was sure this job was it – the answer to the riddle that had tormented me for years. Armed with my research from the library, I was finally ready.

What chance gathers she easily scatters. A great person attracts great people and knows how to hold them together.

— Johann Wolfgang Von Goethe

The Advent[5] element of Water is about alignment with your Desire. It means selection and organization, pooling together resources for use in your greater plan. It also encompasses the concepts of **Energy, Flow and Wisdom.**

The essence of Water is that it flows in a consistent direction. Even when something redirects its path, Water will always go around it. Water comes from many sources, but those sources always collect into a single body.

Water has many purposes. It purifies. It collects in lakes, like pools of knowledge. It effortlessly flows around obstacles and empties into the ocean. We can use this as a metaphor for *collective wisdom and the source of abundance.*

Water is a great example of flow and how it re-adjusts to any obstacles to continue on its path to the end result or destination. Water reflects what is happening to your emotions or spirituality.

Just as rivers, lakes and oceans carry the wisdom of many in a gathering of journey, the force of an area which is a collective of the many equals wisdom. ***Water also symbolically washes and purifies.***

As all water flows to its destination, it collects objects along the way. Many times these are not objects that are a benefit. We, too, experience this in life, and dispelling those things that don't benefit us is the path to purity, just as the waters purify their toxins.

Let go of the past and your paradigms, and then look towards that mysterious Fire inside your core. Take notice where the course of your life has met with turning points. Just as Water turns at a bend in the river, take note of where your course has turned and why. As those reasons become clear, you can begin to let go of the need to repeat the past. You can select better options and align with your desire.

Your life is made up of many scenes, involving many people, places and things that will come and go. They may enter your life for a season or a lesson, or they just may be there for what they are and nothing else. For example, imagine you are a child. Your world consists of family, school, and friends. This is your world, or a scene in your journey. You grow up and change and you enter into another world or scene. Perhaps this next scene contains a completely new environment consisting of a new school, friends, etc. Each scene of your journey imparts beliefs, experiences and lessons (the flow of your life) upon you. These scenes, actors, settings, and experiences all culminate to where you are right now, at this moment. I'm not saying anyone or anything is wrong or right – it just is what it is. Now you are in another scene, or you wouldn't be reading this book. You are in the scene in which you want to co-create your journey moving forward. One element that is certain in this journey, if you haven't noticed already, is change. I am not suggesting you should change who you are, just *re-discover the beautiful person that you are and align with your Desire. It's time to play your part in someone else's scene and start co-directing the next one.*

Identify what you need to move forward on your journey. Include your special talents and the talents of others that can be of assistance to fulfill the quest. Even consider an outsider. An outsider is someone that isn't involved in the current content of your life. However, many times they are the ones that can help provide perspective on the process. They ask the questions like: why do you do it this way, why do you put up with that, etc. They use their paradigm, boundaries, beliefs (which are likely to be different, as they aren't involved in your content) to view the situation. *This is why more than one person to solve a problem will get you better results.* They will add to your flow velocity and the collective wisdom to assist in your journey.

Perceive the Course

Water symbolizes the alignment of your talents and resources with Fire. It also symbolizes the gathering of resources in alignment with any other needs you may have on the journey to your Desire. Perception and your imagination are important influences on your journey. Let's discuss how perception and imagination play a role. Here is an exercise to bring this into clarity.

Perceive: Close your eyes and describe what you see about your Desire.

Imagine: See where it is you want to go.

Think from the end: Put yourself in a state where you feel that you are already there and you've reached the goal. Capture the feeling of it. It's important not to pretend but to go there with your imagination and feel the emotion, feel the experience.

Define: Get clarity on the essential components needed for your success. Know the points, and write them down:

> Where to go in order to be in alignment with your Desire
> What is needed to get there
> How to get it
> When to use it
> Why it matters
> Turning points you can expect along the way

Attraction vs. Distraction

When we talk about selecting what you desire, we're talking about talents or natural attractions to a given activity. They are the things that you are good at or enjoy doing. Many people believe that you can't make a living doing what you like to do. Not only is this inaccurate, ***doing what you love*** to do is the surest path to success. It brings about new opportunities that would not have come about otherwise.

For example, I like helping others. For me, this means listening and facilitating the discovery of solutions, or helping in any way I can and using opportunities to utilize my talents. I enjoy my role so much that I often provide my services for free to those who I feel could benefit but don't have the means to pay. By understanding that my actions were aligned with my path, and not just a career, this has provided amazing opportunities and chance encounters. While doing some pro bono work, I met a professor who was interested in my message and methods. He asked me to speak at his college, and in turn this exposed my ideas to several clients who had the need for my services and had the means to pay. It's important to note that although my actions led to new business, this was a side-effect of just following my path. By *being "in the zone" and doing what I enjoy,* new career opportunities were naturally attracted to me.

You may say you like watching TV, going out to the movies, or engaging in other diversions. At first glance it would appear that you'd have a tough time making a living with your recreational activities. Many times I would classify them as distractions. For most people, this kind of distraction is just that – something to take your focus off of your Righteous Cause. *If what you are doing is not getting you closer to your Desire, then leave that activity behind you.*

To be fair, let's say you may want to be an actor and that may be your passion. Watching TV in that case could be research, and may provide ideas to bring you closer to your desire. Another example could be that movies or tv can provide inspiration, meaning you might observe something during this time that inspires you to a thought or even action. In that case it isn't a distraction but an attraction.

Avoiding Distractions from Your True Course

Life today is so complicated, and most of the complication is due to distractions in our everyday life. *Many of them aren't really all that important,* and just cause us to make decisions based on frivolous concerns. We can wind up making choices that complicate situations even more.

We don't have control over a lot of what comes to us. As much as we can choose the general course of life, there will always be a *random element that can't be contained.* The news of the day, traffic on the highway, the actions of others are all influences on the flow of life. To some degree we can choose which news we take in, which highways we drive on, and which people we associate with. However, ultimately the random element will remain. It's inevitable.

By choosing to take life as it comes, we can stop making things so complicated. *Worry, anxiety, peer pressure, and attempts to please others* can all influence you in negative ways and distract you from your true goal, your Righteous Cause. Instead, if you allow conditions to be what they are, *engage your worries into the Advent⁵ Process,* and let go of distractions, you'll find a deep well of peace and simplicity. The path to your Righteous Cause will be clear as well as free from distractions.

Recognize the distraction when it shows up for you. Understand how it makes you feel, and then let it go. Learn to see what you need to and move on. Don't over-think it. Just allow it to be there and let it go. *Allow this thought process to become your new aligned paradigm.*

Anything you do repeatedly, any thought you think with no effective result, can be called a distraction from your Righteous Cause. You may be distracted by your thoughts that tell you you're not good enough, that you're not adept at anything, or that no one would pay you for what you like to do.

Just as you have dreams, you have talents; God gave them to you for a reason. *Both dreams and talents need to be acted upon to make a difference in your life and the lives of others.* This is your purpose, to serve others and yourself.

Capitalizing on Your Talents

Talents are the *things you are good at and enjoy doing.* You may also find your talents by noticing what others tell you you're good at. Listen to what is going on around you and pay attention to what you enjoy – be the observer. There is nothing so rewarding as getting paid for something you really enjoy.

Make a list of those things you like and those that you are doing that add value to your life. Ask your friends for their perspective, and notice what others are doing that you wish you could, too. Capture all that you can and make a list. Writing it down will help you to make it visual. When we can see and touch something it becomes more real.

Listen to others, and temper their advice with your own wisdom. When people or friends tell you you're really good at something, ***pay attention.*** Perhaps your friends suggest that you should have your own business or they admire your hobbies. This is great feedback, since our emotional attachments often present illusions about ourselves.

Next, review the list, grouping your talents into categories. Ultimately you'll find that your many favorite activities often point to a few basic talents. Don't try to fix your weaknesses but leverage your strengths and talents. Always remember: ***You are not broken.*** You are here in this life to experience its totality, including the mistakes you make and your apparent flaws. The mistakes provide us with valuable lessons, and the flaws give us character. Embrace the totality of your being, and let yourself ***be the person you are.***

Focus on the good that you desire. You have those strengths and talents for a reason, and you were meant to use them. When you align your resources with your desire, all life begins to flow.

This is the foundation of who you are and the beginning of your Righteous Cause.

Recap and Next Steps

At this point, you have seen that the element of Water is about alignment - aligning your thoughts, your talents, the talents of others with the flow of the actions of your Desire, allowing you to fulfill your Righteous Cause. ***Water helps you select your actions and organize collective wisdom.***

Water represents continuous flow. It re-adjusts when it comes to obstacles, continuing on its path to its ultimate destination. In the Advent[5] Process, Water allows us to create a process of flow. We make selections from an array of resources to support our goals. Using the force of Water, we pool our resources to serve as a reserve to draw from.

Water washes and purifies, and it also reflects your emotions. As Water can nourish life, it can also take it. Be alert that Water doesn't submerge your one true aim, your Righteous Cause.

For further explanation and how this process can work for you please visit
www.Advent5.com

Scene 3

Wind

As I sat in the library reviewing the job description, I made the decision then and there to apply for the position and move to Dallas. It was in the customer service department. Even though the job was not within my typical skillsets, I knew that I wanted to be part of the organization at any cost.

The more I thought about it, the more excited I became – the more convinced that it was the right thing for me. This was the answer I'd been seeking for so long. I made a note of the contact information and sent them my resume.

There was just one problem: ***they wouldn't even talk to me.***

A week after applying, I phoned to follow up, make sure they'd received my resume, and schedule an appointment for an interview. The Human Resources phone just rang and then transferred me to voice mail. I left a message. They didn't call back.

When I didn't hear from the HR department, I was concerned that they'd lost my application. These things happen from time to time, so I phoned their offices again to follow up. I still didn't get a return phone call.

I called them again and left another message. There was still no response, even after several days. I phoned again. Then one more time, and again. I knew that whatever problem I was having wouldn't really matter in the course of time. In my mind, the job was already mine. I was thinking from the end and my determination and conviction didn't even allow the emotional and cynical side a chance to manifest.

No one at the company would return my calls. It took me so many attempts to get through on the phone and speak to someone directly that I remember thinking anyone else would have given up long before then. It almost seemed like an accident when I finally did get through. I've come to understand since then that ***there are no accidents.***

Eventually I did reach and speak with the sales manager. "Look, I don't know how to tell you this, but you are way over-qualified for this job," he said. "I've seen your resume. There's no way in the world that you would want to do this kind of work. You'd be gone after the first week. I don't understand why you're applying for the job in the first place."

I told him that I didn't care about any of that, and the money was fine. I told him I wanted to help people, and that I was sure this was the right opportunity for me. I let him know about my own personal history with self-help books and audio programs and how much benefit each one of them had brought to me. The manager was very reluctant, but he knew that if he didn't grant me an interview I would never go away.

We finally set a date for later in the week. I was excited, really looking forward to it, reading everything I could get my hands on about the company. I prepared well for a typical interview.

Still I wasn't quite prepared for what I encountered when the big day arrived.

When the day did come, I met with the sales manager, who was also the head of the department. I answered every question with preparation and ease. Even though I felt like I'd aced the interview questions, he was even more discouraging than he had been over the phone.

He told me he was impressed with my resume, but he also reinforced his point that I was way over-qualified for the position. He said there was no way he'd ever hire me because of that, and he was very discouraging. *I persisted,* and I assured him it would not be a problem. I was quite certain that I wanted the job. I explained that I just wanted to help people, and I knew this would be a great change for me.

By the end of the interview, I could see he just wasn't going to budge. His main concern was that he couldn't see me sticking with a job so far below my qualifications. "I just don't see how this is going to work out," he said.

At this point I knew I had to *meet his resistance head on.* I simply would not give up, even when it seemed that everything was against me. "I understand why you say that, and I probably would be skeptical, too, if I were in your shoes. But do you really think I'd do a bad job? I mean, what do you have to lose?" I asked him. "The worst that could happen is that you'd lose a little training time. That's a risk you'd take with any new employee." He softened a little.

"I'll tell you what," I offered, "just give me a chance. Put me on 90-day probation, and if it doesn't work out, I'll leave immediately – no questions asked, no hard feelings. You really do have nothing to lose, and I might just turn out to be your best employee…"

A light dawned on his face, his head cocked to one side and his shoulders relaxed. I knew I'd won him over. I started work the following Monday.

Leaning Into the Winds of Adversity

Wind is energy. Air represents communication and new ideas. A hurricane or strong wind blows away outmoded thinking from an area and heralds in the new.

You can be pushed around by life's distractions and problems, or you can be pulled by your inner wisdom, your inner self, and the stuff of your dreams. Your inner self is where your dream lives. Wherever you put your focus, the energy will follow. It's been said that your "energy flows where attention goes," which I, too, believe.

The dreams you have aren't yours by accident. They are given to you by God for the purpose of fulfilling them. So when resistance comes, it's your choice. *Will you be pushed around by the Wind of resistance, or will you lean into it?*

The element of Wind can take on many forms. The way you harness the Wind determines whether you let it defeat you or propel you. A sailing ship may harness the Wind in its canvas, or it may be capsized by the powerful forces of nature.

Using the Advent[5] Process, the *Wind can manifest as choices that are healthy* - choices that fuel the Fire of Desire - or choices that are defeated by the overwhelming energy of resistance.

These choices have to do with and include: the food we eat, the thoughts we think, the way we react in given situations, and the way we feel as a result of these choices. We can take steps to improve situations using the momentum of the *Wind to co-create new opportunities.*

In all of life, we encounter situations that can easily be perceived as setbacks. If we let them, they can lead us off course away from the Righteous Cause. Sometimes the shift is incremental, and it can happen day by day. Sometimes the shift is immediate and abrupt. Whether it's a verbal confrontation, a sudden encounter with an old love, a denial from someone we're counting on, an injury, a sudden illness, or even the apparent betrayal of a friend – there are any number of possibilities that can lead to discouragement and take us away from our true aims. *These situations are part of the distraction* or can be the signals to return to the path of your Desire and align with Water.

We all have times when things happen that pull us back into darkness. There will be times when sadness and other emotions overtake you. *Distractions do happen.* They will and they must happen because they are the fabric that makes up your life. You are here in this life to live it as a human being, which means your character and the life you lead are fundamentally imperfect. *Learn to see the perfection in the perceived flaws.* It's these anomalies that build character and give life its richness. Without them it would be difficult to appreciate the wonders of life.

With the Advent⁵ Process, now you have *a path and actions to guide you along the way by design.* When those moments happen and you meet with the Wind of resistance, you can lean into it with confidence and acceptance. The key is to use the Advent⁵ Process to reinterpret the meaning that you give these events. Be willing to view the situation from a new perspective, change your tack, and discover the way to get back on course.

The ultimate measure of a man is not where he stands in moments of comfort, but where he stands at times of challenge and controversy.

— Martin Luther King, Jr.

The 5 Why's

The Advent⁵ Process works even in situations that might otherwise be overwhelming and leave you feeling flattened, like you've had the Wind knocked out of you. The best tool for dealing with sudden, unexpected emotions is what I call the 5 Why's.

Life has a way of dealing unexpected blows. The 5 Why's exercise will help you define the issue and discover where the emotion is rooted, allowing you to develop a sustainable solution. The process becomes surprisingly clear when you ask yourself "why" five times. It's not all that scientific; however, it is effective. In our Process we *welcome issues, problems and imbalanced emotions because resolving them will lead us to greater understanding, strength and wisdom.*

For example, let's say you are judgmental about someone or something. You are feeling pain, and you're unsettled about some situation. You can get to the core of it by asking yourself the right questions and writing down the answers you discover.

When you find yourself in such a situation, ask yourself these 5 questions, with each question referring to your previous answer:

1) Why do I feel this way?
2) Why is that an issue for me?
3) Why does this bother me?
4) Why is this person or thing getting to me?
5) Why is that action upsetting me?

When you find the answer, you will discover that the issue is caused by a deep-seated belief. Understanding the source of this belief will allow you to uncover your belief, paradigm or boundary with a better understanding of how it affects you and others. You can either accept this trait or you can allow it to be transformed into something more effective, useful, and aligned with your Desire. ***The Wind of change can transform you in a profound way.***

Lean into the Punch

Not long ago, I took a trip back to Dallas to visit family and friends. A very good friend of mine had recently lost his wife of 20 years. He and I have known each other for roughly a decade, and we actually call each other "brother."

He and I became great friends when I lived in Dallas, we'd do weekend projects together for the family. Back then, we'd team up on projects during the weekends, we attended family functions together, and he was always there for me when I needed him. So after his wife passed away, I told him I would return to Dallas and spend some time with him before I became too busy with some of the commitments I had overseas.

I decided to take a relaxing trip to Dallas minus the deadlines and commitments of daily life. I flew into San Antonio from Seattle (where I had been working on this book). My daughter and I had lived in San Antonio during her high school years. We had a wonderful time there and it was a growing experience for both of us. That Saturday I had dinner with friends at one of our favorite Mexican restaurants in the neighborhood, and the next morning I decided to take the train from San Antonio to Dallas for a change from the typical airline experience. I was challenging myself to step out of my normal routine. The train took longer than an airplane so it was perfect for reflecting on my life, my book, my journey and my Desire. It was quite fun and relaxing. I was feeling strong and capable.

It was a Sunday night when my friend picked me up from the train station. I'd been spending time in the Northwest, and as my feet hit the train platform, the warm dry air on my face was a refreshing change. Even though my friend had just been through the worst part of his grief, it was good to see him, and that in itself was refreshing.

We went out for some dinner, and the mood was fairly upbeat under the circumstances. I hadn't seen him since his wife's passing, but our conversation that evening was more about two friends catching up than it was about dealing with the weight of his burden. After dinner we went back to his house. There was something important he'd wanted to look at, something he hadn't felt strong enough to do until now, with my support as an old friend. My being there offered the reinforcement he needed.

For some time my friend had wanted to watch the video of his wife's funeral service. Since I was there with him, he finally felt that he could go through with it. We sat in the living room, where they would hang out, with the emptiness of his wife not being there, and he put the DVD into the player.

As we watched the guests file in, the service unfolded as routinely as might be expected for any funeral service. It was solemn without being grim, and my friend seemed to be viewing it with the perspective that a little time can give us all.

I wasn't thinking that much about myself and my own reactions, because I was focused on being supportive of the man whose wife of 20 years had just departed this earth. I knew her, too, and I missed her as well.

For someone newly bereaved, my friend was taking it fairly well. There was a grim relief for the two of us to watch this service together. But in spite of that, or perhaps because of it, I was completely unprepared for the "punch" that this viewing was about to deliver to me. Something happened that left me completely breathless, and the unexpected blow knocked me flat. There was no way I could have prepared myself for what I saw next.

For what I haven't told you is that the woman who passed away was the mother of my second wife, who recently went through a divorce with me. The dearly departed had been my mother-in-law, and my friend had been my father-in-law, my wife's stepfather.

Yet my friend was there for me as much as I was there for him. The fact of my friend's kinship to me couldn't be dissolved by divorce or by death. The bond has been ***tested by the strongest of Winds,*** and we call each other "brother" now as we always have.

The closeness of kin all around at the service was a bit tough for me to see, because I'd been excluded from it. Even though my wife and I had divorced, I still felt a connection with the grieving people I saw on the TV screen. I felt out of sorts because I couldn't comfort them. This sense of being off-balance made what happened next all but unbearable. There was no way to know the punch was coming.

As I sat next to my friend, watching the start of the service and as the family filed in, I saw my recently divorced wife holding the hand of another man. He was comforting her, and it was clear they were romantically involved. It was like my heart stopped and a spear went through it, piercing my very soul.

This piercing ***pain was overwhelming.*** Time stood still, and I began to slip into the same feeling of dark sadness that had consumed me after my wife had asked for a divorce. The pain I felt in this punch stemmed from the sense that she had fully moved on, had completely shunned me, and the familiar emotion of profound significance came over me, the illusion of unworthiness.

As I sat next to her step-father, reeling from the blow, I began remembering the many conversations I'd had with others about the ***importance of accepting and allowing yourself to feel emotions, not resisting them*** but just letting them cycle through. I've coached on this topic for years, and I've had the benefit of others' perspective in casual conversation.

Even as recently as the week before this incident, a friend and boxing coach shared his ideas with me about this very topic. His response to a negative emotion is much like taking a punch in boxing; to embrace it and not reject it, literally ***welcoming the punch.*** His point was that the momentum of the punch can be turned to your advantage, and you can use its energy to propel yourself in the right direction. You can literally ***use the energy of opposition to your gain.***

As it turns out, that conversation was incredibly well-timed, as if forces had prepared me for the difficulties that I would be facing during the trip to Dallas. As if it were planned, the Wind blew another event into this space, a colleague and a friend called me to talk about an upcoming business trip we had together to Montreal. He could tell I was in a challenging state of being and asked what was wrong. I re-lived and ***leaned into the experience,*** we talked, and he gave me a much-needed understanding of the situation. This conversation offered me relief from the pain I was experiencing, I utilized the punch for the positive, and that pain brought me back to the center.

That night, after watching the video of the funeral service, we both turned in early. It had been an exhausting evening for both of us. In the privacy of my own mind, I pondered all that had happened that night.

The next morning I started my routine of meditation and preparing myself for the day, feeling much better after a night's rest and a bit of distance from the event. But if that was the case, then why had the video affected me so deeply? What was the source of the punch here? In other words, what was the root cause of this emotion, and what could I do to release it? I proceeded to use the 5 Why's exercise to get to the core of the beliefs that were limiting me. *You can use the "5 Why's" also when you are faced with the unexpected punch.*

Another gust of Wind came that morning on a call with my publisher. He had called to check on me and see how the trip was going. He is not only my publisher but a friend as well. Once again I re-lived the story but this time it was much easier. During our conversation and with his input, the situation became clear to me. And with the collection of the flow of events and with the acceptance (leaning into Wind) of them it was less painful. But if I had not used these techniques it would have been easy to identify with the situation and go into a complete darkness that I was so familiar with – the path of unworthiness.

As I gained perspective, it became clear that the sadness was not originating from her actions, but it was coming from within me. It was my own small sense that led me to feel so deeply sad by the evidence that my ex-wife had moved on. I'd felt rejected and felt unworthy, a feeling she had never intended to impose upon me. Feeling that way was my own choice. *By identifying the feeling, I was able to let it go and move on.*

Awareness of the Resistance from Within

Sometimes resistance comes from within. The notion of an internal conflict is all too common. In this case, I was able to overcome my own resistance. Like the boxer taking the punch, I was able to leverage the energy of the situation and turn it to my advantage.

Understanding the source of an emotion is powerful in diffusing it. I was careful not to discard the emotions I felt, but also *I chose not to identify with them.* Feeling a certain way doesn't mean the emotion needs to own you. Feeling it and being it are not the same thing. Many people claim to be angry or sad, when in reality they merely feel that way. By choosing a more effective posture about it, it's possible to lean into the emotion without getting swept away by it.

In this case I used this technique to uncover the root cause of the strength of this emotion and why it had crept up on my peace. The key is not to identify with the emotional state but to name it and let it become a part of you, as it is you, and using its energy to move forward. This is truly the essence of *leaning into the Wind.*

It became clear to me that I felt this punch because of my perception of unworthiness. Using the process of the 5 Why's kept me from slipping into darkness. The emotion attached to this event was a reminder of a deep-rooted issue of many years that was so ever present, and not necessarily seen.

How powerful thoughts are…perhaps even more powerful is the fact that we have a choice in our perceptions! *We are not victims of our thoughts,* any more than we are victims of other people's actions or words. *The perception creates the interpretation of events,* and the interpretation creates the emotion. Identifying the emotion allows us to clear it out and choose new perceptions. It's all about point of view and the filters we use in the interpretation.

The greatest gift I got from the punch is an even more heightened awareness of the fact that *we are not broken.* I received a reinforced sense that *everything we need is already inside us.* We are just passing through at this place and in time, with objects and events entering our field of view – a scene, if you will.

Death has an end, and love is everlasting. All form is temporary and the light of your heart will never die, it's here waiting on us. And *it is revealed as pure love itself.*

Lean into adversities. Just as you can lean into the Wind that brings in havoc without asking – without warning - you can lean into those challenging situations and thoughts that are blown into your path. It's how you respond that matters and this is done *by the choice you make to lean into the punch.*

Aligning Your Choices with Your Desire

Wind transforms and propels you through adversity. You can use Wind to expedite your pursuit of your dream, even in the face of adversity. Like the Wind, things can happen in an instant. As you lean into the Wind, you can *be pulled through the distractions of life.*

As with anything in life, you have a choice when you are confronted with resistance. The key is making the ***choice that is in alignment with your Desire.*** As the wind blows, do you automatically follow the course it imposes upon you? Or do you turn the momentum to your advantage? Choose to align your response with your Desire, and you'll experience a better result.

Take a look at your choices and compare them with the results you want to achieve. For example, look at your food choices, thought choices, people you hang around with, the choice of your activities and the way you spend your professional and personal alone time. ***By making a conscious choice, you will have involvement in and with your Desire.***

Criticism is a prime example of meeting the Wind of resistance. If someone criticizes you, they're simply giving you a view of the world from where they sit. By all means don't take it personally. It's just one opinion in a world of opinions. Choose to keep their opinion in perspective. You can use it to find weaknesses in your approach and shore them up. If the critic is simply jealous or trying to tear you down, there can be no harm in what they say.

Don't be offended by criticism. Use the information to help you discover a fresh perspective. In the immortal words of Eleanor Roosevelt, ***"No one can make you feel inferior without your permission."***

Overcoming Your Limits

Setting personal boundaries can be a good thing in managing your interpersonal relationships. It's important for others to know and understand the limits you place on your interaction with them, your social norms, your privacy and other relational factors. In this way, boundaries can be a good thing and a positive force. For example, if you're like most people I know, you have boundaries about people calling you after midnight, eating food off your plate or being too loud in public places. Everyone has certain rules and limits. These types of boundaries are constructive, and there's generally no need to deconstruct them.

However, this is far different from the boundaries of *your limiting beliefs*. In that case, boundaries are not constructive. In fact, they *may be keeping you from achieving your Righteous Cause*. The internal boundaries of your limiting beliefs need to be identified and overcome.

I used to have a boundary about certain types of restaurants. I set limits for myself, choosing only to dine in establishments that were upscale, with linen tablecloths, rich ambiance, and a certain type of clientele.

This boundary limited my options - no other type of place would do for me. I would turn up my nose at any establishment that didn't fit my criteria. I would even go so far as to judge the people who went to restaurants that didn't meet my standards.

Now I ask you… is this a rewarding way to live? Of course it's not! Did I leave myself out of a world of experiences? Yes, I think so. In my choice to limit my dining, I also *limited my*

mind and shut myself out of the chance to enjoy all of life's richness.

By holding onto this limiting belief, I based all my dining decisions on what others suggested that I should want from life. These reactions, fostered in me as a young boy, created a world that I thought was right for me. However, in time I began to dislike the contrived environment of these dining establishments. What I thought was the correct way to behave was actually limiting me and my experiences.

On one of my business trips, I had the opportunity to go to Poland and visit the city of Poznan. My hotel featured lovely fine dining, and the restaurant met with my narrow scope of requirements – the table linens, the food, the atmosphere and even their clientele. Yet after a while, I grew tired of eating at the hotel restaurant, and I ventured out into the city of Poznan.

Poznan is an industrial town that is situated very close to the Polish border with Germany, and the atmosphere is a bit run down. I walked around the town center where many of the restaurants were old and looked poorly kept, without much hope of finding a good meal. They were not places where I would like to eat under any circumstances, particularly in a place I wasn't knowledgeable. I started to get discouraged.

After wandering around aimlessly for the better part of an hour, hunger got the best of me and I selected one of the restaurants at random. It was a restaurant that had been in business since the 1800's. As I walked inside, the first thing I noticed was that the decor was not at all fancy, nor did they have linen tablecloths. The service staff were a little rough looking, and at first I considered turning around and heading back out the door. But something inside me convinced me to stay. I noticed that they all had smiles on their faces, and besides, the aromas coming from the kitchen overtook me. I gave in to my hunger with no idea what was to come.

I asked to be seated and told them this was my first visit to Poland. I wasn't sure about what to order, and that's when the service began. *To my great surprise, I was treated to a richly colorful experience such as I couldn't have imagined.* The waiter explained to me each item on the menu and described how they cook the meal. When I asked which wine he recommended, he took me to the wine cellar, leading me down a long, narrow stairway and into a dark basement.

The waiter shared with me the history of the wine cellar and customs of the restaurant back in the early days of the restaurant. He told me how wine was made there in the 1800s and brought up in small bags that the workers carried on their backs up the narrow stairway. He asked me about the kinds of wine I prefer, and he selected a vintage bottle for me. By this time my meal was on the table and it was time to eat. The food was spectacular and the wine was some of the best I've ever had.

By *casting off my self-limiting boundaries, I was able to open up and enjoy one of life's unexpected gifts.* It turned out to bring me a wonderful time and a treasured memory.

Aligning Your Boundaries for Momentum

In the following exercise, make a list your boundaries. Identify the ones you feel positively about. Also list any limiting beliefs that have appeared, whether or not you understand their origin.

List 5 boundaries/limiting beliefs:

1.
2.
3.
4.
5.

Write down 5 desires, dreams and objectives:

1.
2.
3.
4.
5.

Now list the boundaries you have that will align with your dreams, desires and objectives.

1.
2.
3.
4.
5.

By defining the boundaries that will assist you in your Desire, we can see which ones are constructive and which are not.

Next, let's ask two questions to ensure we have properly defined the Desire and that it's in alignment with what you want. Keeping in mind your boundaries and your Desire, answer these two questions:

What do I want in my life right now?

1.
2.
3.
4.
5.

What, if anything, is preventing this from happening?

1.
2.
3.
4.
5.

Wind can propel you in the direction of your dreams or it can blow you off course. Resistance may come from outside or it can come from within. How you respond to resistance will determine how quickly and effectively you reach your true desire and achieve your Righteous Cause. *You can use the momentum of resistance to your advantage,* letting it feed the flame of your passion without blowing it out.

Recap and Next Steps

At this point, you have seen that using the element of Wind means responding to resistance with renewed commitment. You can use the momentum of opposition to your own advantage. The force of Wind allows you to **make choices that align with your Desire,** knowing when to lean into the Wind, when to leverage your own personal boundaries, and when to let go of them.

You can push through the problems of life and adhere through distractions, or you can be pulled onward to reach your dreams. The dreams you have are no accident. They are given to you so you can fulfill them.

Through Advent[5], you can lean into the Wind of adversity and embrace the periods of life that create stress and find that the **solution to every problem is contained within.** It's all about how we choose to respond.

Wind also represents communication with others and yourself, and it means harnessing the energy of new ideas. It allows us to set up a standard for continual improvement.

Just as in boxing or the martial arts, we use the kinetic energy of the forces that oppose us and turn that energy to our advantage. When we do this, **we amplify our own personal power.** When resistance inevitably comes, will you lean into to the Wind, or will you be blown about like a feather? **The choice is yours.**

For further explanation and how this process can work for you please visit
www.Advent5.com

Sun

After I passed the interview, I went to work for a famous motivational company that I had admired for many years with high hopes and a newly awakened sense of satisfaction. My move to Dallas had gone smoothly, and the change of venue had done me a world of good. Finally, I felt like I belonged somewhere and my work had meaning, plus, an added bonus was that my daughter lived there as well. The fact that my position was in the customer service department placed me in direct contact with the people we were serving as a company. In the world of personal development, this is truly a privileged place to be.

Not everyone has heard of Zig Ziglar, though he is quite well known. At this point it makes sense to give you a bit of context about the man most people would agree is legendary in the personal development industry. Though this book is not about him or his ideas, knowing a bit about him will help put my story into context and address the distraction of unanswered questions.

One reason I was drawn to apply for the job is that I was well aware of Mr. Ziglar's work and his reputation. He started his career as a salesman, and he enjoyed remarkable celebrity as a motivational speaker and author. In fact, he won the respect of peers and fans alike. His writing was first published in 1975, and he wrote over 30 books before his death in 2012, when he was mourned by millions. What made him so beloved was his quick wit and his folksy common sense about complex life issues. On his audio programs, his Southern twang lends an intimate nature to his sometimes tough advice.

Searching the name Zig Ziglar on Amazon.com yields more than 1,300 products, and a Google search delivers more than 2 million results. He was almost as prolific as he was talked about. Being able to go to work in the morning for a company so universally beloved was a great satisfaction for me.

My background in sales and as a consultant had given me the skills to work effectively with the general public. I never had any doubt about that, nor did my new boss. My job in customer service for Ziglar was easy enough to learn, with few moving parts. There wasn't much to it – talking, listening, and helping people solve their problems. It put me on the front lines, placing me in contact with the kind of people who not only needed help but also welcomed it. That factor alone is rarer than you might believe.

I focused on the process of learning my job and carrying out the tasks of my position. I was settling into a routine, *performing as reliably as the Sun coming up in the morning,* and through this my career seemed to blossom on its own. My focus allowed me to experience more than I could have imagined.

What happened is that in the course of time, my manager's initial skepticism turned to trust and finally enthusiasm about my addition to the team. He and the president of the company saw that I was doing something different, and they wanted to know more about my background.

I received an honor that placed me in daily contact with Mr. Ziglar himself, working and traveling with him side by side. I'd taken the job because I'd wanted to help people. Pursuing the Fire of my Desire was about to reward me in spades.

A project I became involved in was to assist in building a legacy for Mr. Ziglar and his company. He went deliberately about the task of leaving a legacy for future generations to access and benefit from. I helped define and execute the project's objectives.

One of our successes was to create a college freshman course for defining and reaching goals. We found that the biggest reason students drop out of college is that they have no direction and fail to see the bigger picture. The legacy project used Mr. Ziglar's programs as the basis for a college course in goal setting that increased academic retention at one university by as much as 65%. Becoming involved in this project, I was definitely doing what mattered and making a difference.

Even after my time with the Ziglar Corporation **there was still emptiness, one of lack of fulfillment.** So I returned to my consulting business. I was still searching, however, with a totally different perspective and wisdom that gave me solace.

Legacies are carefully built – they're not automatic. Leaving a legacy is something that requires thinking of a larger picture, something that's bigger than life itself, and a span of time that extends far beyond the present. It takes vision and an expansiveness to consciously choose what the world will remember you for.

People who leave rich legacies are aware of the importance of the richest asset of all – wisdom. Leaving a legacy means imparting skills and life experience to others. When tomorrow comes, this day will be gone forever; in its place is what we have left behind. We all have the ability to leave a legacy. Using the Advent[5] Process, you can decide for yourself what that will look like for you. *What triumph will you leave behind?*

As Constant as the Rising Sun

Applying this element of the Sun means changing your behaviors and having them align with your Desire. The Sun means focusing your activities on the Righteous Cause and transforming your routine with a measure. *It's about focus.*

The sun follows a set path, rising every morning, setting each night, and there are predictable changes from season to season. The sun offers light to illuminate your path. *The Sun offers focus on your path and your intended activities.*

In the Advent[5] Process, *the Sun represents consistent application.* It means a standardizing of the path and changing your behaviors to align with your Desire. The Sun lets us put measures in place to ensure success of the Righteous Cause.

Wisdom is gained by interpreting past experiences and beliefs, by acknowledging that our experience is subject to our interpretation, and recognizing that with hope we see differently than others see. By looking through the lens of hope, we see a way to transformation. By assessing our activities and making refinements, we are *focusing our efforts on achieving the desired outcome.*

Just as the energy beam of Sun can illuminate a dark room, we can focus our energy in a specific arena. We can transform our old routines that aren't beneficial and align with the newly found Desire, talents, and choices.

The path will be standardized, guiding us to follow the new patterns, and we can measure and gauge our progress. This allows us to adjust to situations that arise from the distractions of everyday life and continue to flow toward our chosen intended manifestation. *There is always a way – always.*

After applying this element, we can maintain focus on the things that really matter and eclipse the ones that don't.

The Sun wins the battle against darkness and rises again. The Sun is the star around which all other celestial bodies of the system revolve. *Without the attraction of the Sun, the planets would be mere lifeless matter drifting through space,* so the Sun is the light that determines the direction and the purpose of the planets. This is also true with us. The Sun will provide the focus and the path of the journey to our Desire. It also provides the process for moving forward to the future with a defined present.

Think with the end result in mind. A dream imagined clearly and acted upon in the present with expectation will always evoke the circumstances and power necessary to bring about its own manifestation. It doesn't matter how unpredictable, unlikely, or even impossible those circumstances may have seemed before.

Change your thoughts to focus on the object of your Desire, and you will allow all the forces to align for you with abundance.

Stretching yourself means doing something that is outside of your accustomed beliefs and boundaries. If your core passion rests with something you don't believe possible, then go for it anyway. Your only limits are your thoughts. You don't know what opportunities the act of commitment will bring into being – and you won't know until you commit.

To practice, start simple. Pick something that is possible only if you give it focus. Then work your way up to something that will have a large impact.

The ability to concentrate and to use your time well is everything if you want to succeed in business--or almost anywhere else for that matter.

— Lee Iacocca

Balance and Well-Being

In the previous section, we discussed the exercise of the 5 Why's. We found that we can drill down to the core of deep-seated beliefs and emotions, and discover the source of conflicting or ineffective emotions. The Advent⁵ Process gives us a method for dealing with such newly uncovered discoveries. Take a look at the following 5-step process and following actions.

1. Ego: Don't personalize. Even if you feel it's a personal attack, it isn't about you.

2. Awareness: Step back and take time to get a view of how the event makes you feel and why you feel the way you do. Happiness and negative thoughts cannot coexist.

3. Allowing/Accepting: Stop the resistance, including resisting the anger or negative emotion about the issue. Just accept that it is what it is. It has happened. Now what should you do?

4. Alignment: Which solution or response adds value and is in alignment with your desires, life, goal, objective and the vision for yourself?

5. Choice: Which path shall you take? Typically you have two paths: internalize or make the best of the situation. Another option may be to do nothing, just allow it to be.

Suggested Thought Process:

- ◆ Ensure the steps/actions taken are towards the vision
- ◆ Plan and map out all activities and compare to objective
- ◆ All thoughts are aligned with vision
- ◆ Take the time to consider your thoughts that benefit the steps you need to take
- ◆ Evaluate all actions
- ◆ Remove distractions; clear clutter in mind and body
- ◆ Pursue objectives
- ◆ Be here now
- ◆ Use your creativity and imagination

Thoughts lead on to purposes; purposes go forth in action; actions form habits; habits decide character; and character fixes our destiny.

— Tyron Edwards

Thoughts and Emotions

What are you focusing on? Your thoughts create your actions and, therefore, your reality. Emotions are your inner communication, the signal to your mind of how you feel about something. What you focus on determines your behavior.

All the subjects we've discussed so far relate to the topic of how we communicate to ourselves and others. *All of the boundaries, values, beliefs, and distinctions that you possess serve to create your inner dialog.*

When someone near you is happy and laughing, it's difficult not to begin to feel the same emotion they do. This comes about through their vibration – the frequency they are sending out.

All of life and matter is vibrating, by the very nature of the sub-atomic particles within their cells. The rate of the vibration can be modified through thought and emotion. The higher the vibration, the more positive the emotional experience. Being around someone who is laughing serves as a tuning fork for you own frequency. Often you can't help it!

What's even more powerful is that you are attached to your own emotions based on your beliefs and past experiences. More often than not, these boundaries dictate how we see life, the movie you play in your head of you, and they strongly influence our decisions. They give us a specific point of view. The thing is, *we have a choice as to how we interpret those experiences.*

If we focus too greatly on a single point of view, we can and will miss other possibilities to solve a problem, to make the best decisions to move forward. We may even choose to stay in situations that aren't healthy for us or ignore the uncomfortable. Coupled with the vibrational state you are in, these two forces – thoughts and emotions - may work to your advantage or disadvantage. *Once again, the choice is yours to make.*

When you focus directly on something, truly concentrate, you don't notice what is going on around you. There are many methods of focus meditation: prayer, self-talk, communication with your higher self. What you focus on is where your energy goes. If you communicate about a given topic, this is where your energy goes, even if you don't like the conditions surrounding that topic. With the attention you give it, you bring even more of the same vibration into the situation.

The *things that separate us may be turned to our advantage* through the simple choice of focusing on their opposite. Where you are obstinate, choose to be flexible. Where you meet your own ineffective boundaries, beliefs, opinions, teachings and definitions, choose to replace them with thoughts that bring about a higher vibration, a positive energy of sorts. You'll know you've succeeded when you begin to feel lighter, happier, and more at peace.

The Sun always wins the battle against darkness to rise again. In reality, the Sun is always there. It is only our perception that it has ever gone away. Much like the love and light that is within you, it never goes away, we just disconnect from it. This is why when we focus on our Desire with the alignment of the other elements, it seems simple and things fall into place – only because *it is already here, and always has been. This is why it's easy.* By applying the Advent[5] Process your light will begin to shine and illuminate your path.

Staying On Track

As you connect with the Fire of your Desire and define your action steps to achieve your Righteous Cause, standardize your new routine and remain focused on your tasks with consistency. This will allow you to *remain on the path and provide you with the ability to measure your progress.*

With this standardized routine you have identified using Advent[5], and with measures you put into place, you will have a better mechanism to adjust your behaviors and keep in alignment with your Desire. *Everything is a process.* You have the choice of which path your life will follow.

Processes are great if they are designed in alignment with your essential self and the destinations you want to reach. We all have choices, so *choose deliberately in alignment with your Desires,* focusing on the activities you know will take you where you want to go.

Recap and Next Steps

At this point, you have seen that the Sun is the star around which all other celestial bodies revolve. The attraction of the Sun means that the planets are not mere lifeless objects wandering through the void, but heavenly bodies moving on a set track with an elegant purpose. The Sun is the gravitational force that determines the direction and movement of the planets.

So it is with us. In the Advent[5] Process, the ***Sun provides the pull, the focus and the path of our journey to our Righteous Cause.*** The Sun means centering, focus, direction and alignment of your path. The Sun transforms darkness into light, helping us to change our behaviors to align with our desire.

With the Sun, we maintain focus on the things that really matter, and we eclipse the ones that don't. We transform thoughts and emotions to serve our highest needs, and we ***choose the ones that serve our grand design.***

For further explanation and how this process can work for you please visit
www.Advent5.com

Rock

I knew my commitment to helping others had paid off. I was truly using the Fire of my Desire. My "whatever it takes" attitude had vaulted me beyond my expectations; my passion and commitment served as the foundation of my new career.

I am blessed to have had many opportunities to have experiences that have colored my perspectives. I was able to make a decision, devise a plan in alignment with my passion, execute it in spite of resistance, and maintain focus upon it. The result is that I laid the foundation of a career with deeper meaning than I'd ever known before, one that might transform the lives of others by following my own Righteous Cause.

It was during this time that I first began to form the ideas that would become Advent[5]. All of the processes and parameters seemed to gel for me. All of life seemed to crystallize into a higher perspective, one with a grander view, yet a complete grounding in the fundamentals. *Life is truly a process,* and interacting in this lofty capacity within the personal development industry, I felt as if I were standing on a mountaintop and all of life's flow was at my feet.

Recently, while I was having dinner with my family in Dallas, we touched on the topic of this book and the Advent[5] Process. I found myself becoming more and more animated during the conversation, so much so that as I spoke the entire restaurant around me became silent. I was aware that all I could hear was the sound of my own voice. It was strange, almost distracting, to observe how strongly I felt and the focus upon my Righteous Cause was so powerful. My words were interrupted by the ***volume and depths of my own passion for this message.***

If you have built castles in the air, your work need not be lost; that is where they should be. Now put foundations under them.

— Henry David Thoreau

Standing Your Ground

The element of Rock is about ***commitment, willingness and sustaining.*** Rock embraces the "whatever it takes" attitude. The Rock is your foundation and the essence of the unwavering dedication to your Righteous Cause.

All facts are the result of something, some process, and your dreams will change your results. Your dreams fuel your activities, and through your deep dedication to your Righteous Cause, you can refine it and see it through to fruition. Whether you succeed with your first attempt, recognize that ***there are no failures but only results.***

When we look into our dreams and actively participate in the journey, the results we experience and co-create will provide a firm footing and a sense of ownership. With ***ownership comes consistent commitment and the willingness to do whatever it takes.*** This is how we sustain our new path. We build new life on a foundation, a foundation that is strong because we built it ourselves, the authentic self. It's not something that was imposed on us from the outside but created from within.

Rock is solid, but it can change form. If you get stuck in the mud, it can show you where you are in your life. Likewise, an earthquake tells you that the foundations of your life are not as secure as you may have thought. From Earth there is new growth, such as mountains and valleys. Rock is about finding yourself on the plateaus, standing firm and enjoying the vistas. The ***Rock is a symbol of our strength, commitment and consistency.*** Rock also provides us with a certainty of the willingness to have all of our Advent[5] elements at anchor to sustain the renewed alignment with your Desire.

We know that everything is a process, and you have the choice of what process your life will follow. ***Processes are great when you choose the process that is in alignment with who you are and where you want to go.***

Rock is also about assessing your plans, ensuring that the process will yield the desired result. We all have choices, and when you follow a process - any process – you create your own experience. With Advent[5], you have the deliberate means to design your life with a proven system.

The element of Rock allows you a place to soothe your soul by laying the foundation and returning to your touchstones. With the security and peace of mind that the Rock brings, it's possible to let the love in… for that is the ultimate goal. No other aim could be higher than peace of mind, and that only comes by ***fully understanding where you've come from, where you're***

going. It comes from knowing that where you've always been is precisely where you were meant to be. It is only with your applied imagination – the sense of ***allowing yourself to pursue your life's passions – can you have the peace of mind you seek.***

A rock pile ceases to be a rock pile the moment a single man contemplates it. bearing with him the image of a cathedral.

— Antoine de Saint-Exupery

Sustaining the Desire

Rock is strong and resilient. It is able to withstand Water, Wind and Sun. Rock is the foundation upon which you sustain your Desire, as it is the ownership to make the consistent commitment to do whatever it takes. ***This can only come from within – not from any outside sources.*** The magic of Advent[5] is to transform your Desires into a rock-solid system of results which you can measure, track and monitor.

When you are in alignment with your Desire, you will do whatever it takes. No sacrifice seems too great. That can be missing something that you so looked forward to, eliminating unnecessary pieces of your life puzzle, or going beyond what would seem like the ordinary call of duty. ***Discover the Unseen… and you will find it mysteriously placed in your path.***

What are the actions that fit your Desire, the Desire as you defined it? Perhaps it will become very clear why you are where you are. If the place you are now is not where you want to be, analyzing your action may help you come to understand what's keeping you from standing on solid ground. Take a look at the routine activities you need to pursue and sustain in order to achieve your Righteous Cause.

Rock is about ***making choices about your future in the present,*** working with the end in mind, and sustaining your activity until the desired outcome is reached. It sounds easy enough to do, but sustaining the right activities has proven to be one of the most difficult tasks in this Process. Not only does it require persistence to keep in alignment with the other process elements, but you need to stay in the present moment to drive your choices to ensure that your current actions will drive you toward the end result.

Being willing to do whatever it takes is crucial. First take the time to define your Desire and follow these systematic process steps. By following these steps it will become very clear what you need and what is needed to accomplish your Righteous Cause through your Desire and live the life you were meant to live – live on purpose.

Recap and Next Steps

At this point, you have seen that Rock provides us with a symbol of the certainty of our will. It anchors the other elements as the symbol to sustain your alignment with your Desire. ***Rock represents our strength, commitment and constancy.***

Rock is solid, strong and resilient. It can change form, such as when an earthquake tells you that your foundations are not as secure as you thought. It is also able to withstand Water,

Wind and Sun, so Rock is about sustaining the process as well as sustaining your desire. ***Rock provides the sense of ownership that enables commitment to doing whatever it takes.***

Rock means refining your choices to keep them in alignment with your desire. It provides a firm foundation that will stand the test of time.

The magic of Advent[5] is to ***transform your Desire into a rock-solid process yielding results*** you can measure, track and monitor, returning again and again to your cherished touchstones to gain a sense of peace.

Advent[5] is an action-driven, results-oriented process by which you participate in the design of your life. The number 5 represents our life path, change and freedom.

For further explanation and how this process can work for you please visit
www.Advent5.com

Conclusion

You will never find time for anything. If you want the time, you must make it.

— Charles Buxton

It is understandably human to see yourself as small. The only way to stop feeling insignificant is to see beyond the flesh. We are spiritual beings having a human experience. At our very **core is the ultimate Spiritual Being**, and that is the life force of our existence.

We are pure energy, infinite, inexhaustible, and irresistible. As a creation of this Source, all is within the reach of your power. This is where your Desire and your Righteous Cause reside. When we align with that power within, **we reveal the authentic self** and enjoy all the abundant facets that life has to offer.

The alignment begins with discovering your true Desire and your talents. They are alive within you because they are the very gifts that God has given you. All we need to do is remove the day-to-day noise and listen. Listen to what our heart is telling us, look beyond appearances, and **welcome what we see with our hearts**. It starts with awareness of Discover the Unseen…

When we find that when we are in alignment with these components, our life happenings become easier, events and emotions fall into place. Our attitudes, fulfillment, sense of happiness and sense of peace ***all come from living the journey with love.***

The Advent[5] Process can give you profound insight into what lives in the core of your heart. This isn't to say that everything in your life will be perfect or without upsets, conflicts, or even perceived disasters. We need all of those experiences, because they make up who we are and guide us to where we need to be.

Who Put the "God" In Goderich

I was on one of my many trips to Canada one July, and on this trip I found myself on the shores of Lake Huron in the small, beautiful town of Goderich, Ontario, a town dubbed by the Queen of England as "the most beautiful town in Canada." I was working a two-week project, and the town was so peaceful I decided to spend the weekend.

I went to the farmers market on Saturday and walked to the waterfront. I walked among the many booths and chatted it up with the local vendors. Later that day, after the market had cleared out of the town center, I decided to sit on the park bench and do some writing and much-needed reflecting. I was thinking about giving up on my book, and I had much to ponder about my life in general.

After I sat on this bench for an hour or so, I saw a man walking through the park, and I became a little defensive. I didn't like the way he looked, and, in fact, I jumped to the conclusion that he was going to try to ask me for something – money, cigarettes, it didn't matter. I didn't want him intruding on my private reverie. With my boundaries firmly in place (I guess I didn't learn enough from my Poznan experience), I pointedly ignored him – at least I thought I appeared to ignore him. But in my mind, all of my focus was directed on the path of his steps.

As you might imagine, the intensity of my focus seemed to magnetically lure him to sit on the bench right next to me. Though the park was full of benches and there wasn't another soul in sight, this man came deliberately up to me and said "hello."

I put down my notebook and pen and said hello. He asked what I was writing, and I told him I was working on a book. He asked me for more details, so I thought to myself, *"God is always talking,* so I'm going to engage in conversation with this man." I opened up and let down my reserve.

The first thing that happened is that he put out his cigarette and apologized for the smoke that had blown in my face. It was as if the small opening I offered had let him in.

We talked about my book and he said he, too, was a writer. My initial reaction was one of skepticism, but I realized my judgment wasn't serving either one of us. I stopped myself in mid-thought. In fact, I let go of the assumptions I'd been making about this man and I asked him about his book. I fully listened to his reply as he explained that he had a book published, and that he was happy for a while. But his challenge was his drinking, and he lost everything because of it. Now he was just trying to get back on his feet.

He never asked me for money or anything else for that matter. We talked for more than an hour, and I never once felt that he wanted anything from me but to talk to me about the task of writing. Our conversation wound down, and he gave me a big grin, looking me in the eye meaningfully. He encouraged me to keep writing, shook my hand, and off he went. His words touched me just at the right time. I made the decision to take his advice and keep writing.

Anyone might have had such an encounter in an empty city park with no one around. But the thing that made this chance meeting so pointed is that as he walked away through the open city square, I glanced at my journal for only a moment, just long enough to write a sentence. When I looked up, he was gone, not a trace of him in sight. I've long wondered how it was that he disappeared so completely and quietly.

Accept the present moment and find the perfection that is deeper than any form and untouched by time."

— Eckhart Tolle

Suggested Beginnings

As you move through the Advent[5] Process, start simple to practice. Pick something that is possible only if you give it focus. With success under your belt and faith in yourself, work your way up to something that will have a larger impact on you and your life.

Dealing with variations, distractions, noise and interference will likely be your toughest challenge at first. Once you have identified those things that interfere with and distract you from your inner self, you will be more likely to *find the places, people and energy that match your Desire.* You can and will make choices about your environment and people you associate with that are far more effective than they have ever been. All these ideas, concepts, processes and the tools we've discussed and applied will lead you down the path of your Desire.

Don't hesitate to act. We choose inaction at times because we spend so much time trying to figure out how we are going to do something. Inaction may also come from believing that it can't be done because the way doesn't seem clear. *Do what you can with your God-given talents with the situation you have at this point in time.*

With the defined desire you need direction. Remember that *intention sets the direction.* It's very important to have a direction in mind, but also to remain flexible and open. It's crucial that you have defined your direction before you get into action, but don't let fear of failure keep you from acting at all. Your results will provide you with the feedback you need to know whether you're on the right course.

Go confidently in the direction of your dreams. Live the life you have imagined.

— Henry David Thoreau

Below is a method and process steps to help guide you in the journey along the way, a set of suggestions, reminders to keep you focused and ensure your direction.

Beyond the First Effort:

◆ Keep the commitment
◆ Renew body, mind and spirit
◆ Expect ongoing changes and revelations
◆ Be gentle with yourself
◆ Help and serve one another
◆ Where attention goes, energy flows
◆ Keep a journal
◆ Practice daily affirmations
◆ Be consistent
◆ Have a confidante
◆ Make a sacred contract with your essence

The Fabric of Your Being

It has been said that the silence between the notes is what makes the music. So goes the silence that is within you. That is God, your soul, the essence of who you are. This is the essence of who we are as a community, company or society. It's the whole point of life.

You are all of what you are. There is no separation, you are connected to all that is, and you are part of the one God. You may think that you have two aspects, one good and one bad. The truth is you are all that you are made of.

There's just you and your need to understand and use those parts to your benefit. You are given all the components that make you who you are at this moment. You can't resist them or try to get rid of the so called "bad." All aspects are a part of you and have a defined purpose. It's when you *Discover the Unseen...* that you find the answer. *You're not broken.* You are exactly who and where you need to be at this moment. Be grateful for all that you are, and embrace, allow, accept all that is presented to you, including your greatest Desire.

The happiness you seek comes from the peace of knowing that you're not broken. The things that happen for you make up the fabric of your life and make you the wonderful person that you are. Know that there is no separation, and we are all one of the same Source.

It all begins when you *Discover the Unseen...*

A note from the author's perspective:

Even writing this book has been a process with the use of the Advent[5] ideas/concepts/processes and tools. The book that started out as a business book has transformed as I defined my Desire and the message I intended to deliver. The process has transformed into *a book of discovery, enlightening and challenging myself.*

On Martin Luther King, Jr., Day, my publisher and I attended a breakfast honoring King's life and his Righteous Cause. The speaker was a roommate of MLK in college, and shared insight and stories of this icon. He was a man that embraced all the elements and essence of Advent[5] – to live his Righteous Cause.

After the breakfast my publisher wanted to meet with me and discuss the book and the progress, as it had been a week or so since we had seen each other. We went to a nearby hotel in downtown Seattle on the water and sat in the lobby by the fireplace to review. We spent hours discussing the message, as I wasn't satisfied. The message as a business book was not enough. Something was missing. We continued to talk and brainstorm as people would slow down and listen in to what we were discussing. Working through my thoughts and frustration it became very clear that we needed to change the direction of the book. An idea came to my publisher and what I had been sharing about what I felt the message should be – with a smile on his face he shouted out "it's all about a Righteous Cause." At that moment it became very clear to me, yes, that was the purpose of my message, and the message of the book. *It is all about living your Righteous Cause through your Desire – living on purpose.*

We discovered that we weren't dreaming big enough, we weren't building a bigger foundation; we weren't changing the rules, nor were we releasing our limiting beliefs and boundaries. We weren't listening to our Desire for the message and I wasn't challenging myself to step out of my normal routine either.

After that meeting on the waterfront in downtown Seattle, everything began to fall into place. It was my Desire to deliver the message of the process of self-discovery. It's the path of discovery in each and every one of us to fulfill our Desires.

Everyone and everything we have needed for the book, tour and business has shown up for us. Not to say we haven't had periods of doubts, but whenever we returned the focus to the path of our Desire and applied the Advent[5] elements, it became easy at times. I believe it was *easy because everything we need is already here.* That's why it's simple. Everything has been here waiting on us to rediscover or reconnect. We also found that everyone that has decided to join our journey is equally excited and ignited for living their Righteous Cause as well.

Looking at the simplicity of the Advent[5] Processes and the path that lies ahead, we are getting closer to happiness and joy. What an honor it is to share these ideas, concepts, and processes that lead people back to their Desire. The passion and the enjoyment of doing something with meaningful experience associated with abundance and Love is indescribable. This is available for each and every one of us. All that is needed is the removal of the distractions and to reconnect with your authentic self, all of this being your Desire, and the *Love for yourself and others.*

As you build on your foundation with Desire (Fire), with your talents (Water), with joyfully leaning into the adversity (Wind), focusing on your selected path (Sun), and with the solid commitment (Rock), you'll *find power and joy* on your way to living your Righteous Cause.

Uncovering your authentic self and aligning with your Desire in living your Righteous Cause will generate a feeling of purpose and completeness. I know this, as it has happened to me in the process of completing this book and the development of the processes of Advent[5].

We look forward to being part of your journey and helping in any way we can. Remember, it all begins with a process to *Discover the Unseen…*